Catch Them
if
You Can!

Catch Them
if
You Can!

How Any Manager Can Win the War for Talent in the Global Labor Shortage

GREG FORD
&
DR. JOHN SULLIVAN

Author of *Rethinking Strategic HR* and
Improving Productivity the World Class Way

iUniverse, Inc.
New York Lincoln Shanghai

Catch Them if You Can!
How Any Manager Can Win the War for Talent in the Global Labor Shortage

iUniverse books may be ordered through booksellers or by contacting:

iUniverse
2021 Pine Lake Road, Suite 100
Lincoln, NE 68512
www.iuniverse.com
1-800-Authors (1-800-288-4677)

Because of the dynamic nature of the Internet, any Web addresses or links contained in this book may have changed since publication and may no longer be valid.

The information, ideas, and suggestions in this book are not intended to render professional advice. Before following any suggestions contained in this book, you should consult your personal accountant or other financial advisor. Neither the author nor the publisher shall be liable or responsible for any loss or damage allegedly arising as a consequence of your use or application of any information or suggestions in this book.

ISBN: 978-0-595-48401-0 (pbk)
ISBN: 978-0-595-60488-3 (ebk)

Printed in the United States of America

ACKNOWLEDGEMENTS

Sage advice, zealous encouragement, fearless criticism, eagle-eyed editing—these are some of the much needed ingredients that others provide authors in the creation of a book. First and foremost, thank you to Master Burnett for the enormous amount of effort he put into making this a better book. Without his talent, this work may not have been published. Thanks also to Addie Sullivan, Allison Ford, David & Grace Aplin, Michael Bacchus, Cam Macmillan, Marian Ford, Lana Okerlund, and Michelle Wilson for the cover design.

Thanks also go out to some of the authors who over the years have popularized the narrative business-book format, authors such as Robert Kiyosaki (*Rich Dad, Poor Dad*), Spencer Johnson and Ken Blanchard (*Who Moved My Cheese?*), Patrick Lencioni (*The Five Temptations of a CEO*), Robin Sharma (*The Monk Who Sold His Ferrari*), Michael Gerber (*The E-Myth*), and many others. As well, this book incorporates some tenets of creative ethnography from qualitative researchers such as Dr. Elliot Eisner, Dr. John W. Creswell, Dr. Carolyn Ellis, and Dr. Arthur Bochner, and some of the story-based learning methods of people like Dr. Roger Schank. If you enjoy this story, it is due in part to their admirable pioneering efforts in their fields.

Contents

INTRODUCTION

This is a story of a group of managers seeking to end the seemingly constant stress on their work and family lives caused by not having a sufficient number of high-quality workers. This unique group of managers was frustrated with the kind of advice and help they were getting from their overburdened human resources departments. They knew there must be a better way and as a result, they were determined to solve this problem once and for all by committing themselves to a journey to find the answer to their problem. This story covers their journey toward a new attitude, a new mindset. It includes a variety of interesting characters and a plot that contains both the high and low points of their search. If you, as a manager, are also tired of losing your daily battle to attract and retain the very best employees, we urge you to follow along with the adventures of your compatriots as they seek out and eventually find "the answer."

CHAPTER 1

The Journey Begins

<table>
<tr><td>Chapter 1 Learning Points</td></tr>
</table>

1. An inability to find talent is restricting the growth of many organizations.
2. While talent exists, getting to it requires persistence. Organizations now have to beat a path to the door of the talent versus the talent beating a path to the organization.
3. Top performers can be hard to find, and they tend to be busy working. They generally don't have time for idle chat.

"A journey of a thousand miles begins with a single step."
(Lao-Tzu)

Once there was a group of friends who had grown up together and still stayed in touch at monthly breakfast meetings. They were all managers within their companies, and they each faced a similar problem: they couldn't find workers—never mind "top talent"—for their companies.

These managers tried all the usual methods. They worked with their human resource departments to put job ads in their city's daily paper. They posted openings to Internet job boards. They set up booths at campus career fairs. Some had engaged the services of recruiting firms, with varying degrees of success. But still they were understaffed and the people they did attract were not always star performers. The result was that work was piling up, products were not getting shipped, customers were being lost. The managers were stressed, and their personal lives were suffering, too.

My name is Peter, and I was a member of that group. As a vice-president of sales for a software company, I had a phenomenal career and results were limited only by my inability to attract and retain the best workers.

Sitting in my office late one night, looking at the picture of my family that I kept on my desk, I suddenly remembered something. I couldn't believe I hadn't thought of it before. At a birthday party for my uncle several years earlier, I had met an old friend of his. The man was, from all reports, *the* guru in recruiting and had been headhunting the best-of-the-best for Fortune 500 companies for decades. Companies waited in line for his services not just because he was an excellent recruiting consultant but also because his approaches and tools were both innovative and easy to implement.

I turned to my computer and sent an e-mail to my friends, suggesting we try to find this "Tiger Woods of recruiting." Like me, many of them were working late, and their enthusiastic replies came back quickly: Let's track this man down!

We soon found out that he had recently retired and had become a bit of a recluse. But we also learned that he was still helping a few top companies develop recruiting strategies. Word was that the man put people through a series of games and challenges in a recruiting boot camp of sorts. I was determined to secure the services of this recruiting guru, no matter what hoops or games he might put us through. The problem was that nobody knew how to find him.

I called the headhunter's old firm but nobody there seemed to know where the man now lived. I found the man's home number in the phone book, but his number had been disconnected. On hearing the news, half of our group said, "Well, I guess that's that. We'll have to give up on finding him." The quick departure of these individuals left only five of us to continue the hunt for the reclusive King of Headhunters.

> The road to recruiting top talent contains many roadblocks and a great deal of misleading advice. Successful managers don't quit at the first roadblock or misstep.

Not being one to give up easily, I decided one Saturday afternoon to invest several hours trying to track this man down. I found the old address of the ex-recruiter and knocked on the front door. The new residents did not know where the man had gone. I visited the neighbors, but they, too, had no information. A call to the realtor who had sold the man's house reaped nothing. "Sorry," said the realtor, "but the proceeds from the sale went into his bank account, and that's the last I heard from him." I was about to hang up when I thought to ask the realtor if he knew which moving company the man had used. Several calls later, I was speaking with that company's driver who, nearly a year ago, had moved the man's possessions to a cottage near a lake a hundred miles to the northwest of the city. The driver could not remember the exact location of the cabin but said that someone in the nearby resort town would surely know who the man was and where to find him.

The end of the following week saw a holiday long weekend approaching, so the five of us made plans to drive up to the resort community and find the man, hoping to at least engage his services on a contract basis. When the Thursday night came, we hopped into two vehicles and made the two hour drive, stopping only in the resort town itself to fill up with gas, get directions to the man's nearby cottage and to grab a hamburger at a fast-food place. We all laughed as we ate our burgers under the large "Now Hiring, All Shifts" sign prominently hung over the external dining patio. It seemed like *everyone* was having recruiting problems.

The last few miles were down a bumpy, gravel road with dense brush on each side. We passed several cabins then turned off the gravel onto a dirt road near the end of the lake, a track that led to a well-kept cedar cottage with a shiny new SUV parked in the driveway. Smoke puffed from a chimney on the roof, and several blue jays berated us from a nearby picnic table.

At last, as the sun was setting over the lake, the group of us stood outside the cabin door and looked at each

A recruiter for a large regional bank headquartered in the Midwest made 31 calls in 31 days attempting to have a conversation with a potential candidate. The candidate finally called back, stating that she was only returning the call because the recruiter had demonstrated that he would not stop calling until they had a chance to talk, and that all of his messages had been professional.

other, as if each one lacked the authority to actually knock on the door. I finally stepped forward and knocked. For a moment it appeared that nobody was home, but then we heard footsteps thumping across the hardwood inside. The heavy wooden door opened and before us stood a man in his early sixties, his six-foot two-inch frame attired in a cardigan sweater and worn blue jeans. He removed his reading glasses, pushed back his graying hair—which could have used a trim—and sized the five of us up. He scowled, cocked his head to one side and, in a rich, deep voice, said, "I'm not interested." He slammed the door behind him and we heard a bolt slide into place.

We looked at one another. Even the blue jays were silent for a moment as if waiting to see what would happen next.

"Let me try again," I said, as I knocked once more.

"I said I'm not interested!" came the shout from within the cabin. "Go away!"

"What do we do now?" someone said.

"We go back," said another, throwing her hands up. "This was a complete waste of time." She piled into her vehicle with her road partner and the two of them roared off, saying they'd see us back in the city the following week. That meant that seven out of the original ten had already given up the crusade before they even talked to this guru.

The other three of us stood around for a moment longer, staring at the cabin as though there might be a second, more amenable, retired headhunter inside who hadn't emerged yet.

"Let me try one more time," I said. I stepped onto the deck that wrapped around the cabin and gingerly walked around to the front of the building. I looked through an open, screened window into a small sitting area, and to my surprise, there sat the recruiter in an armchair with a glass of lemonade in one hand and a book of crossword puzzles open on his lap. A black Labrador retriever lay sleeping at his feet.

The man looked up at me and chuckled. "You've just passed the first test," he said. "Go get your friends and come on in."

This is the story of how a fellow named P.D. Hawkston, one of the world's best headhunters, helped us save our companies.

* * * * *

Recruiting is very much like Sales (but with a crummy budget). Before you can close even the simplest deal, you need to accept the fact that there will be conflict and rejection along the way.

CHAPTER 2

Here Comes the Eighteen-wheel Truck with No Brakes

Chapter 2 Learning Goals:

1. Educate yourself about the labor crisis. Organizations now are having difficulty finding people to fill seats, let alone finding top talent.

2. Labor shortages or wars for talent do a lot more than make hiring a headache; they impact the business by delaying service to the customer, limiting the volume of business that can be accepted, and more. Learn to analyze the impact a worker shortage will have on your business. Learn to forecast talent needs for your organization.

3. Great managers realize the changes in the market and go after the talent versus waiting for the talent to come to them.

> *"We cannot solve our problems with the*
> *same level of thinking that created them."*
> **(Albert Einstein)**

The breeze off the lake, cool and refreshing, lazily entered the screened windows of the cottage's front room as we sat and chatted with the man who insisted we call him Hawk, "cause everyone calls me that … friends and enemies alike," he said with a laugh. The dusk light from outside, and a light over the kitchen stove, helped the fireplace illuminate the room. I could see a wall of books behind a desk with a laptop on it. Several paintings and prints were hung about the room, classy touches offset by a large stuffed fish mounted over the fireplace and a Green Bay Packers cheese-head atop the television set.

Hawk's dog lay peacefully on the hardwood floor beside him. Our host explained that the dog's name was Scraps, a tribute to the fact that nobody at the pound had wanted the mutt when Hawk saw him there several years ago.

After asking after my uncle, Hawk invited us to tell him about ourselves. We explained that we had originally set out to find him as a group of ten, but that seven of our friends had given up in frustration. Hawk didn't seem surprised, but he was clearly pleased with the perseverance of the three of us.

My pal Dale, sitting in a faded armchair that blended with his worn grey sweatshirt, told Hawk about the construction company he owned that consumed most of his life, and the six kids who consumed what was left. Dale, who was built like an overweight linebacker whose glory days had passed him by twenty-five years earlier, always had a mischievous twinkle in his eyes, despite the worry lines permanently etched above them that were due to the growth of his company.

Sue-Lee explained that she was a partner at a prestigious public accounting firm in the city. Her words were clipped and sparse, as though she wasn't sure if she trusted the stranger before her. She mentioned that her husband, a cardiologist, was also acutely aware of the difficulty in attracting and retaining skilled professionals. Together, they had two teenage girls, both honors students at a private academy. "I also run marathons on the side," she concluded. I noticed Hawk raise an eyebrow at

A famous sausage manufacturer in the Great Lakes region, after learning by accident that sociable line managers from other areas of the business did well in recruiting, established a professional recruiting function staffed solely by professionals with previous line experience. Within seven months of forming the new group, manager satisfaction with recruiting had improved by 37%, cost-per-hire had been reduced by 22%, and turnover of new hires during the first 90 days on the job had been reduced from 4% to less than 1% at a time when the company nearly doubled its headcount.

this. I couldn't tell if his expression was one of *Wow! That's amazing,* or *Lady, you don't impress me much.*

When it was my turn, I described how the software company I worked for had twenty offices across North America, and how our sales had quadrupled in the last three years. I mentioned my two sons, ages nineteen and fifteen, and that my wife was a social worker for the government. I omitted the fact that I hardly saw my kids because of all the overtime I was working lately, and my wife was angry at me for recently postponing a planned family vacation.

Hawk nodded at us and frowned thoughtfully as he took all this information in, seeming to process some questions to which he alone knew the answers. Finally, his face dissolved into a warm smile and he sat back with a sigh. "Now, what can I tell you about myself?" he said. He explained that he had studied economics and psychology in his undergrad years at Cornell University, and had gone on to earn an MBA from Northwestern. He had held several research jobs early in his career before stumbling into a position with a large HR consulting firm. One job led to another and he had ended up specializing in recruiting, going on to become one of the most successful executive recruiters in the country. He rambled amiably for a while, mentioning some of the top companies he had served over the years before retiring.

"Do you miss it?" Dale asked.

"Sometimes," Hawk said, leaning back in his chair. "But I wouldn't trade this for anything." He motioned across the lawn to the lake and the beautiful pines towering over us. He told us about the fish he'd caught and the birds he'd sighted, and how the lake community was a great place to retire and recharge, especially after his wife had died three years ago.

"I suppose I'm glad to have some company," he said, as he walked over to his small kitchen area and began pouring lemonade. He explained that, every once in a while, an executive or two would arrive from the city and ask him for help in recruiting staff.

"Do you always pull that 'hard-to-get' act when people arrive?" asked Sue-Lee. "After all, two of our friends are headed back to the city as we speak."

Dale pulled a cell phone from his pocket. "We could call them back."

Hawk held up his hand. "Nope. The first thing you're going to learn is that persistence pays off. Every time you try to recruit a top performer, he or she will probably blow you off at least once and maybe several times. They don't have time to talk with you."

"But you ended up talking to us," Dale said.

"Sure. Every single person out there will *eventually* talk to you if you're persistent enough. If you don't have that—what do they call it—that 'stick-to-itiveness', you'll never be a good headhunter."

We all looked at one another. "We're not here to become headhunters," I said. "We're all managers in our companies. We leave recruiting to HR."

"I see," said Hawk. "You're not recruiters. You're extremely busy, big-wig managers. Then tell me, why *are* you here?"

> In the United States, growth in the transportation industry will create 504,000 new jobs for drivers while the talent pool to fill those jobs will shrink by more than 490,000, creating a projected net shortage of 994,000 drivers according to data from the US Bureau of Labor Statistics.

"We can't find enough employees?" said Dale.

"We can't find enough *great* employees," Sue-Lee said. "Our firm is looking for the top performers out there, but we can't seem to find them."

"And when we do find the top performers, we often can't catch them," I added, "because they've got two or three different offers on the table." I explained that twenty sales consultants worked in my division, but that I would hire another five if I could find qualified, experienced people. What's more, my company was looking to fill at least sixty IT positions nationwide. And we weren't alone. Job opening statistics showed that, just seven years after the tech meltdown, IT companies were again crying out for talented people.

Sue-Lee shared my problem. Accounting firms across the country were desperate to find junior accountants. Sue-Lee and her partners were prepared to add at least ten in their local office alone if they could find them.

Dale possibly had the biggest challenge. He owned his own company, a huge industrial construction and trucking outfit with more than seven hundred people working on multi-million dollar projects far and wide. Despite his good ol' boy image, Dale had ulcers and got only about five hours of sleep per night due to the worry of his job. Both the construction and transport sides of his business would be in trouble if he could not find enough skilled employees in the years ahead. He shared a staggering forecast: there were 3 million professional truck drivers in North America and 17,980 drivers would be retiring or exiting the industry *each month* by 2012.

And the three of us weren't alone. The newspapers were filled with stories of companies desperate for skilled workers. The U.S. Department of Labor predicted a shortage of 10 million American workers by the year 2010, with the healthcare, manufacturing, energy, and public sectors experiencing the greatest shortage. The consulting firm Watson Wyatt predicted that Canada could face a shortage of 1.2 million workers by 2020, meaning that one out of every thirteen jobs will be vacant!

> The United States National Aeronautics and Space Administration (NASA) projects that colleges in the United States will only graduate 198,000 students with degrees in science and engineering to replace more than 2.1 million science professionals exiting the workforce by 2008.

I mentioned that the famous management guru Peter Drucker has suggested that the convergence of the aging population and a shrinking supply of youth is unlike anything that has happened since the dying centuries of the Roman Empire. I also brought up a book called *Impending Crisis*, which bluntly stated that the labor shortage will reach "crisis proportions" and that few executives really comprehended the risk to their bottom line. "The book argues that high employee turnover can cause bond ratings to drop and stock prices to tumble, threatening capitalization." I felt compelled to add that even if we somehow found enough workers, they may not have adequate technical skills. I was about to mention other issues like outsourcing and an aging workforce, but I didn't want to sound overly alarmist.

As we shared our stories, Hawk rose and stoked the fire. Soon, an orange glow warmed the room, while outside I could see that the skyline above the trees was almost dark. I thought I glimpsed a bat flitting past the deck.

Finally Hawk sat down again and released a heavy sigh. "There is no question about it. There is a talent shortage coming down the mountain like an eighteen wheeler with no brakes, and most people are standing in the middle of the road with no clue where to run. It's going to be a huge dilemma. One expert is calling it the Worldwide War II for Talent."

"Why Worldwide War *two*?" asked Dale.

"The first was the huge hiring boom in the late nineties, largely driven by the tech sector in certain pockets of the U.S. and Canada. But this next one will be massive and will be global."

Prepare for a Global War—Although the war for talent in the late 1990s was mainly restricted to the US and Canada, that will all change this time around. Already firms are facing severe talent shortages not just in the US and Canada but also in Australia, Ireland, the Middle East, and around the world. Labor shortages are already occurring in Malaysia, India and China, countries that for centuries have been enjoying a surplus of labor.

We silently absorbed the impact of what Hawk was saying.

"How come the public didn't see this coming?" I finally said.

"We did," answered Hawk. "The Bureau of Labor Statistics in the United States has been tracking statistics about the workforce for more than 50 years. Early news stories predicting our current demographic crisis emerged in the 1980s, and continued to highlight the projected shortages throughout the '90s. But it wasn't until 2002 that the projections started to attract worldwide attention. Dozens of newspaper and magazine stories commented on this very subject."

He walked over to his oak bookshelf and pulled out several archived magazines. He thumbed through pages marked with yellow sticky tabs, opening each one to a relevant story. "This issue of *Business Week* says that 'focused as they are on today's problems, most companies aren't looking too far around the bend. But when they do, they're in for some big surprises. As the economy strengthens, say demographers and economists, labor shortages will come roaring back.'"

He held up a more academic-looking report. "This article from the *Monthly Labor Review* says that there are 78 million baby boomers—that's you—in the US workforce. You make up 26% of our population and a whopping 54% of our workforce. Many boomers have already turned 55 and are taking early retirement."

"And there's not enough people to take our place," mused Dale. "Hmm … I have always said I'm irreplaceable."

"What about our kids, this Generation Y I've heard about?" I asked.

"They're coming. The front end is just entering the workforce in entry level jobs now. But there are only 60 million of these Gen Y'ers—also called Millennials—compared with more than 78 million Baby Boomers exiting the other end."

> In his landmark book *Boom, Bust & Echo*, Dr. David Foot says that over the next five years more and more baby boomers will be heading for the exits. By 2012, the boomers will start turning 65, and we will see a mass exodus from the labor pool like never before.

"Perhaps Dale should have had more kids," I joked, referring to the six he already had.

"Dale's family is a tiny drop in a big empty bucket," said Hawk. "Our fertility rate has been steadily dropping for decades. A whopping 43% fewer American children are being born today compared to fifty years ago. All of these factors translate into a massive labor shortage, plain and simple."

"That's scary," Sue-Lee said quietly.

Hawk leaned toward the fire and stirred the coals. "Why scary?" he asked her. "What is your biggest fear?"

"What do you mean?" asked Sue-Lee.

"What happens if you carry on like this for the next five or ten years? What happens if you can't fix this problem?"

Dale let out a grunt. "I'm screwed; that's what happens. Goods won't get shipped. Our construction projects will fall behind. There'll be cost overruns. I'll lose existing customers and future bids to companies or countries that have solved the talent problem."

Hawk stared at him. "And what happens then? What is your biggest *fear*?"

After a moment Dale responded quietly. "I could go out of business." Heads nodded all around.

I spoke up. "If I can't find sales people to help meet our revenue targets, I'll lose my job." I almost added that if I kept working crazy hours I would lose my family, but I fell silent instead.

> **Warning: Turnover Ahead. The US, Canadian and worldwide statistics on the upcoming talent shortages report only *half* of the problem that individual companies will face. As the economy improves and the unemployment rate drops, external job opportunities for those that have been "stuck" in jobs for the last three to five years will begin to open up. As these employees gain confidence in the growing economy, they are likely to quit their jobs at an alarming rate. In fact, smart managers should prepare for the fact that turnover rates are likely to nearly double in the next two years from their low in 2004.**

"What about you?" Hawk asked Sue-Lee. "Will you lose your job? Will your accounting firm go under?"

Sue-Lee shook her head. "Probably not. But we won't be able to deliver on client projects, we'll start to look incompetent and innovation will certainly come to a halt."

"So your biggest fear is that you'll lose face. It's a status thing with you, is that right?"

She cast a resentful look at him. "That's rather harsh, don't you think?"

Hawk shrugged. "There's no right or wrong answer. Everyone's fear is valid. You may not go out of business, but you may see shrinking profits, or you may become exceedingly stressed out, or you may look bad in the eyes of customers, or many other scenarios could emerge. But one thing is certain: if you can't find good employees, you're in trouble. No matter how fast technology develops, having great people will always be a critical success factor for any firm."

We sat in awkward silence for a while. We stared at the sparks and flames that Hawk, softly humming a tune, was again stirring up in the fireplace. The smell of birch smoke drifted pleasantly through the warm room, as we started removing our sweaters and jackets.

Out of the blue, Hawk asked how old we were.

"We're all forty-eight," Dale said.

"And how long until you retire?"

"I don't know about you guys," I said, "but I plan to work only another seven or eight years. I just hope I can hang on until then."

"Easy for you to say," said Dale. "I own the company. I want to leave it in good shape for my kids to take over." He paused for a moment, then chuckled. "But I guess this will be their problem then, not mine. I'll be sitting on a beach in Florida, drinking margaritas and listening to Jimmy Buffett."

"That is the mantra I'm hearing from many people your age," said Hawk. "There is an army of you leaders in your late forties and fifties who are marching—no, sprinting—as fast as you can to retirement, hoping to get there before the bottom falls out."

A manager at a multi-national electronics firm who had consistently been one of the harshest critics of his corporation's recruiting department realized one day that no larger business problem existed beyond the firm's inability to fill critical positions quickly. In the fast-paced electronics industry, a vacancy in a key design role could cause delays in getting a product to market or mistakes in the design process that could cost the company millions of dollars each day in lost revenues. Recruiting immediately became a business problem versus a functional problem.

"I don't know about that," said Sue-Lee, shaking her head. "I care about my company."

"How much do you care?" asked Hawk.

"A lot. I helped build it to what it is today. Do you think I want to see my legacy fall apart? Do you think I want to leave it in shambles?"

"Probably not. But are you willing to do almost anything to help the company?"

"I have for twenty-five years," she said proudly.

"Good," Hawk said, looking her straight in the eye. "Then you're now a headhunter."

* * * * *

Consider the consequences—Failing to effectively recruit both the quantity and quality of talent that you need can have numerous negative impacts on a business. Some of them include:

- lower employee productivity
- loss of customers because you can't fill orders
- slower product development
- higher turnover rates as your frustrated employees leave
- severe limitations on your ability to grow the company.

Chapter 2—Manager Action Steps

Some suggested actions for proactive managers include:

✓ **Be afraid**—Do some additional reading on the war for talent, the aging workforce, the skill gap and the inevitability of global competition. Use that fear as a heads-up to inspire you to become a talent expert before your competitors do.

✓ **Calculate business impacts**—Work with your CFO to calculate the business impacts of having numerous position vacancies, low new-hire skill levels and the resulting low productivity due to the aging workforce, the skills gap, and the global competition for talent. Some of the possible negative consequences of failing to have the right people in the right jobs include goods not shipped on time, low product quality, lower customer service ratings, projects falling behind, loss of existing or future customers and even an image of instability or the rumor of going out of business.

✓ **Integrate recruiting into business processes**—It's important for managers to realize upfront that no one will be exempt from labor shortages and some industries will be hit especially hard in the war for talent. It's critical that you integrate great recruiting and retention into every business, measurement and reporting process.

✓ **Forecast talent needs**—Develop a process for forecasting your talent needs. Work with budgeting, sales forecasting and strategic planning to get some idea of where your business is going and what your talent needs will be in the next 18 months.

✓ **Prepare for increased turnover**—Assume that your turnover rates will increase dramatically. Put someone in charge of retention tools and efforts but make all managers accountable for turnover. Focus on the turnover rates of top performers. And, especially if you are well known as an employer of choice, prepare retention and "blocking" strategies to minimize the damage from competitors' raids.

✓ **Identify your "talent competitors"**—Because companies within commuting distance may compete with you for talent and non product-specific jobs (talent competitors are generally different from your product competitors), know your enemies. Do a side-by-side comparison of what tools and approaches they are utilizing and compare them to yours, so you can counter and top each one.

✓   **Look ahead**—Monitor the indicators that tell you when competition for talent is increasing so that you won't be surprised. Indicators include: changes in the unemployment rate, job growth rate, economic growth rates, low employee-engagement scores, changes in the number of applications received, the "time-to-fill" for your own jobs, and increasing vacancies and turnover at talent competitors. Major mergers, layoffs and facility expansions should also be monitored as indicators of future changes in the talent picture.

CHAPTER 3

You're *All* Headhunters

Chapter 3 Learning Goals:

1. When recruitment fails, it is the client manager who suffers; therefore, managers must own recruiting.

2. The reality is that managers are hiring the best talent they can from whatever pool their processes produce. If your processes produce mediocre talent, you are hiring the best from that mediocre pool.

3. Realize that world-class recruiting is a 24/7 activity, not a periodic event. Make recruiting your day-to-day responsibility, rather than just an HR duty. Educate your executive team on the need to be heavily involved.

4. Understand the true importance of recruiting and the return on investment that top talent can deliver for you.

"First 'who' then 'what.' Get the right people on the
bus before you figure out where to drive it."
(Jim Collins)

A log in the fire cracked, and a spark jumped onto the floor in front of us. Dale, Sue-Lee and I started, but Hawk just kicked the ember back toward the grate.

Sue-Lee looked baffled at Hawk's last remark. "What?! I'm supposed to be a *headhunter* now?"

"You're *all* headhunters. Whether you like it or not, recruiting will be one of your top priorities from now on."

Sue-Lee folded her arms across her chest. "Maybe our human resources manager should be here instead of me."

> **The Difference between a Recruiter and a Headhunter**—Corporate recruiters tend to be less involved than external headhunters because they are on salary and get no special reward for hiring top talent. As a result, they are relatively passive and often focus on the administrative aspects of recruiting. They recruit during the day and then go home. In contrast, great headhunters are warriors (hence the name) who get huge bonuses for success. Because they have "skin in the game" headhunters don't see their work as a 9-to-5 job. Headhunting is an integral part of their lives and they are constantly identifying, building relationships with, and selling top talent on their job opportunities.

Hawk's voice became quieter. "Your HR department is not getting the job done, is it? Otherwise you wouldn't be here."

"They do a good job in HR," Sue-Lee said. "It's just that they have so much to do, and we have so many openings to fill. I thought that by coming here I might learn some other way our organization can do things. Perhaps a new way to re-structure our old processes."

"That's just it. You're talking about fixing a broken system," exclaimed Hawk. "Instead, you need to throw out the old system and build a new one. The people in HR are well-intentioned but you have to realize up front that managers and even employees must 'own' recruiting because they are the ones who suffer when it's done incorrectly. HR, although concerned, cannot really understand your needs or the impact on the business if they do a mediocre job in recruiting. When recruiting produces weak results, the people who suffer must take charge of it."

"That sounds a little radical," Dale mumbled.

"Of course it's radical. But desperate times call for you-know-what," Hawk said. He began telling us about a former MIT professor named Dr. Michael Hammer, who has been called the father of re-engineering. "Hammer says that in the new business revolution, companies can't tinker and fix, but have to start over, to re-invent themselves around processes."

Suddenly the phone rang, but Hawk just reached over and pressed a button, letting his answering machine kick in.

"When it comes to the process of finding employees," he continued, "almost every company needs to rethink its hiring methods. Too many companies are stuck in the old days when they opened the cattle gates and the cows stampeded toward them. Companies could take their pick of the herd back then, but not anymore.

"But we offer them great opportunities," Sue-Lee protested. "Isn't that enough?"

"Well, let me ask you this," said Hawk. "If you are starving, do you stand at the gates of the pasture, stare at that one cow out there and say, 'That cow sure is lucky that I have this hay in my hand. I hope she walks over here sometime'? Or do you put on your boots and go after the cow?"

Sue-Lee's lips curled up in a tight smile. "You have a way with words, Mr. Hawkston."

"I do my best," he replied, crossing his legs. "Great recruiting is putting on your boots and going after people. In good economic times, potential employees have numerous choices. If you don't pro-actively seek out potential applicants and vigorously

A multi-national software firm realizing that future generations were driven by different ideals undertook a dramatic restructuring of how work was assigned and managed. They started by determining what future generations were interested in from an employer and reverse engineered a project-centered work-allocation model that enabled incoming top talent to literally write their own job descriptions and offer letters including such elements as narrow descriptions of what type of projects they would work on, how many hours a week they would contribute, what benefits they wanted, and where the work would take place. While this notion may seem complex and unmanageable, the software giant made it possible by embracing the same management systems that have been in use at professional service firms for many years. In other areas of the business where utilization of top talent didn't make economic sense, the software giant invented new tools that enabled individuals without application specific education to accomplish what once required specialized skills.

try to sell them on your job, you will end up with the dregs and numerous unfilled positions."

I sighed. "The balance of power has shifted."

"You're darn right," Hawk said. "Remember Tom Peters, the former Stanford professor and McKinsey partner who wrote *In Search of Excellence* back in the early eighties? He wrote another book called *Re-imagine*. In it, he talks about a 'Brand You World.' He says that big companies no longer rule and employees don't have to genuflect on command. Workers have been liberated, and the good ones know they are in demand. So if your prospective hires have picked up on this, you're going to have to go after them."

"You're talking about poaching staff from our competitors," said Sue-Lee. "Doesn't raiding employees go against business ethics?"

"In the new war for talent, no. In fact, I'd say that your fiduciary responsibility to your company includes finding the best employees to help drive profits."

Dale looked thoughtful. "We need to take ownership of recruiting as *our* responsibility, that's what you're saying. And it doesn't matter whether we're hiring nurses or welders or bus drivers. If they report to us, or directly impact our jobs, then we have to become individually accountable for recruiting them."

Hawk gave us a look that confirmed this.

Sue-Lee was still defensive. "I can see that it's becoming more important, but I'm a partner. My focus isn't on recruiting."

Having your CEO accept responsibility as your chief recruiter is rapidly gaining adoption across a wide range of industries. A CEO at one of the largest hotels in Las Vegas stood up before all 7,000 of the property's employees and declared that one of the company's primary objectives was to recruit and retain the best hospitality workforce in the world, and that he would lead the charge. Since that date, the CEO has scheduled blocks of time each week to chat with top candidates in hard-to-fill and mission critical positions. In addition, he has made it a point to meet candidates personally who interview for high growth positions and who currently work for a competitor. Overall, offer acceptance rates have significantly improved, as have operating margins. A portion of the increase in performance has been attributed by the CFO to an increased caliber of workforce.

"Then you're going to have a big problem," said Hawk, matter-of-factly. "Because I assure you that if you don't start spending more time wooing top talent, your competition's managers will have a field day, because they are out there recruiting already."

Dale winced. "I don't know. I'm with Sue-Lee. I've got a lot on my plate."

"Is that right?" said Hawk. He sat back and gazed out at the black expanse of lake. "Bill Gates spent about a quarter of his time as CEO of Microsoft flying around the country to meet with potential stars and their spouses, explaining his vision for the new hire's role in the company, trying to convince that top talent to work for him. And Microsoft did all right, didn't it?"

"Not bad, I guess," chuckled Dale.

"Gates always said that his best business decisions had to do with picking people. You can learn from that. Most high-achievers are extremely goal oriented, possessing an unparalleled desire to win. And that includes winning top talent."

"Jack Welch was like that, too," I put in, recalling the former General Electric CEO's autobiography, *Straight from the Gut*, that I'd recently read. "He said that it wasn't him that made the company so successful, but the people he hired."

"But a good company still needs one leader who is the brains behind the operation, right?" Sue-Lee asked. "Someone who has a vision and can get others to execute it?"

A small regional healthcare organization realized that hiring great people required a great partnership between line managers and recruiting. They set out to create a "Candidate Bill of Rights" that outlined the role of all relevant parties in securing top talent and set forth a standard for the experience each top candidate should be guaranteed. Demonstrating their faith to the partnership, recruiters and line managers alike proposed that a portion of their compensation be placed at risk and be awarded solely on their performance at providing the desired experience as measured by a predetermined set of metrics. The firm, which once had a vacancy rate as high as 29%, now maintains one of the lowest vacancy rates in the healthcare industry at 4.7%.

Hawk waved his hand. "That's a flawed model called 'the genius with a thousand helpers,' according to Jim Collins in his book, *Good to Great*. The great companies Collins studied were all led by savvy CEOs who aggressively raided the best and the brightest people, enlisted their ideas, and then let them loose to run the show. Those leaders got the right people on the bus—and the wrong people off the bus—and *then* figured out where to drive it."

I cleared my throat. "It's easy to pay lip service to that. But how involved do those CEOs actually get? I know a few who only meet with the final shortlisted candidate, almost as if to rubber stamp that person."

"Many of the top bosses are like that," Hawk said. "But I'll wager that the CEOs of most successful companies are *very* involved in staff hiring and retention."

"Any examples?" Dale asked.

Hawk nodded. "The CEO of one medium-sized bank in Ohio felt that recruiting was so integral to the company's success, that he invited the head of recruiting to make a presentation at the annual shareholders meeting. The presentation emphasized how critical recruiting was to increasing shareholder value."

"Well, sure," said Sue-Lee. "People are vital to the company, not fixed assets."

Hawk held up a cautionary finger. "Let's take it one step further and say, 'The *right* people with the right skills in the right jobs are your most important asset.' That distinction also comes from the book *Good to Great*."

"That's a no-brainer," chimed in Dale. "Of course our best people are our best asset."

Hawk sighed. "Most managers blithely recite that litany, but in most cases it is pure lip service. If employees truly are the number one asset, then finding employees should be the number one priority … or at least in the top three. But I can't tell you how many times a recruiter will send great resumes to a hiring manager only to have the resumes sit unnoticed for days or even weeks. Or, a candidate will show up for an interview and be made to wait for fifteen or twenty minutes. Or, after the interview the candidate will not hear back from anyone for weeks. These actions send a message to applicants that hiring great people is well down the priority list. Companies don't treat prospective customers this way, so why do they treat prospective employees like that?"

The three of us quietly contemplated our own companies' recruiting performance. I sensed Hawk's gaze on us, and felt as though he had plunged a dipstick into our collective managerial prowess and pulled out a reading that was disappointingly low.

"You keep talking about 'top talent'," said Dale. "But in today's tight labor market, there are more nags than thoroughbreds."

"Not true. That's an excuse that many hiring managers will offer up because they don't know how to find and sell the best performers. Top talent is out there everywhere, including right under your noses. You just have to find them, sell them on your opportunity and then keep them happy."

"Keep the *best* people happy," I clarified.

Hawk sat back and nodded. "McKinsey & Company issued a report a few years ago that emphasized the need for companies to pay more to top employees to retain them. A company's top performers—the 'A' players—are 50 to 100 percent more productive than average or underperformers. 'Even if you pay an 'A' player 40 percent more to retain him/her,' the report stated, 'your investment yields a 300 percent one year return on investment.' It's the same thing we see in sports and entertainment."

> In sports, Recruiting Is King. Sports is a field where everyone understands the value of top talent in winning. Look at the 2004 Los Angeles Lakers. They lost a coach and just one key player (Shaq)—just two people in a huge organization. And in one single year they went from being a participant in the championship game to a team that didn't even make the playoffs. In sports, it is absolutely clear that recruiting top talent is the key to success. No one in the organization is exempt from constantly looking out for, and helping to lure, top talent to their franchise.

A murmur of understanding echoed among the three of us.

"Finding and keeping top performers is absolutely one of your highest priorities in the years ahead," Hawk continued. "Welch has a great line in his autobiography: 'Losing an A is a sin. Love 'em, hug 'em, kiss 'em, don't lose them!' Welch explains that GE holds its managers accountable every time they lose an A employee. Take a guess how many A's they lose in a given year."

"I'll bet it's less than ten percent," I ventured.

"In fact it's one percent," stated Hawk. "How's that for outstanding retention?"

"Not bad," I murmured.

There was silence for a moment before Dale spoke up cheerfully. "Well, after that speech, I guess I'm a headhunter and a retention manager. Where do we go from here?"

Hawk laughed and stood up. "There are a few motels along the beach in town. Go get some sleep now so you'll be well rested when we start tomorrow."

"When we start what?" Sue-Lee said, her voice rising in uncertainty.

"The training program. Isn't that why you're all here? To learn how to find top talent?"

We stared blankly at him. Finally I spoke up. "I think we were just looking for some tips or tricks of the trade. And I heard that **you** helped companies develop overall recruiting strategies." I realized I **had no** clear expectation of *how* this gentleman would impart his wisdom.

Hawk nodded. "I *will* teach you about developing recruiting strategies for your companies, something I'll wager you don't have now. It's difficult. It involves a complete change of mindset."

"That's good," Dale said. "Peter could use a new mind."

Hawk laughed. "What I teach is not so much how to become a headhunter. Instead, what I'll teach you is how to *think* like a headhunter—that's the key. The difference is that top headhunters have a candidate-centric point of view, while employers have a job-centric point of view."

"But doesn't the headhunter work for the employer?" I said, confused.

"Of course. Make no mistake; the headhunter's first allegiance is to the client, the employer. That's who pays his or her fee. But to deliver the new hire, they have to focus on the pool of candidates and identify the best fit."

Dale sat forward. "I get what you're saying. The headhunter has to have an employee-centric mindset to best help the employer. That's what you teach."

"That's it," Hawk said. Then he stood and clapped his hands. "So, if we're going to do this, I want you here for breakfast at seven in the morning. I'll have activities planned for the entire day. It will be almost like a one-day boot camp. From now on, you can call this place Camp Hee-Ho-Head-Hunt-Ha."

"Hey, I like that," chuckled Dale. "*Camp Hee-Ho-Head-Hunt-Ha.*"

Sue-Lee did not laugh. She looked outside at the night sky, and I could tell she felt uncomfortable about how this was shaping up.

I spoke on her behalf. "Thanks, but perhaps we can just get together for a lunch in town tomorrow, and, you know … pick your brain a little."

Hawk dismissed this idea with a wave. "It's been picked over like a ham bone in a dog pound. The *only* way to really learn this stuff is to do the activities I have planned."

"We couldn't impose," I tried again.

"You're not imposing upon me," grunted Hawk. "If you want to learn anything, you *have* to take part. That's my only condition. Otherwise, see you later. It's your choice." His face then softened a bit, and he smiled. "Besides, I make the best omelet you've ever laid your lips on."

We looked at one another again. Dale shrugged and gave me the same look I had seen a thousand times, the one he wore just before he was about to do something mischievous that he knew he might regret later.

"I suppose we could give it a shot," Dale said.

I had to ask the question. "Hawk, how much … umm … what kind of consulting fees are we talking about here?"

"You mean, what I charge for the training?" said Hawk. "Don't worry, it's mice feed compared to the problems you guys have. I'll send you the bill."

"Can we afford your recruiting expertise?" said Sue-Lee with a little laugh.

"You can't *not* afford it," replied Hawk. "Not if you want your companies to thrive."

"What kind of training program is it?" asked Sue-Lee warily. "I'd like to know what I'm getting myself into."

"Spoken like a true bean counter," he said. He went on to explain that we would be playing a game. The three of us would compete against one another, each winning points for how well we did at challenges and tests he assigned. At the end of the day, the one with the most points would win the contest.

"Win what?" asked Dale, sitting up like a kid who'd been told there was a shiny trophy on the line.

"That's a surprise. You'll find out Sunday morning."

"What kind of challenges are we talking about?" asked Sue-Lee. "They're not physical, are they?"

Hawk stood and walked over to the fire, where he reached on top of the mantle and grabbed a small metal can. "Don't worry, everyone can complete these tests. They'll be fun." He started sprinkling water on the fire, and it began hissing and smoking, dying for the night. "For now, it's time to get a good night's sleep," he said. "The contest begins tomorrow."

Dale looked at me and in a taunting voice said, "Hand me a twist-tie, 'cuz this game is in the bag."

On the way to the motel, we used our cell phones to call home, telling our spouses where we were and when we'd be home, but leaving out the details about what we had gotten ourselves into.

If we had only known.

* * * * *

Chapter 3—Manager Action Steps

Some suggested actions for proactive managers include:

✓ **Change the roles**—It's important to realize upfront that the role of recruiting is shifting from HR to managers. Job descriptions, measurement systems and performance goals must be revised so managers and employees "own" recruiting. Everyone must develop the mindset of a headhunter.

✓ **Change HR's expectations**—Because great recruiting needs to be done close to the actual work, it's essential that managers increase the amount of time and budget that they spend on recruiting. Simultaneously, it's important for senior managers to work with HR to ensure that they understand that HR's role must change. Their role must shift from a "doer" to an expert consultant on effective recruiting tools, strategies and metrics.

✓ **Make it 24/7**—Rather than being a periodic "event", recruiting must become a continuous process. The expectation must be that it is on the mind and the agenda of every manager (and every employee) every day. View recruiting as a constant process, even when there are no position openings at the present time.

✓ **Calculate the performance differential**—Work with cost accounting in order to calculate the value of a top performer in your own organization. Compare the difference in performance between a top performer and an average performer where it is easy to measure output and quality (example: sales or customer service). McKinsey & Company reported that a company's top performers—the 'A' players—are 50 to 100 percent more productive than average or underperformers. The report states: "Even if you pay an 'A' player 40 percent more to retain him/her, your investment yields a 300 percent one year return on investment."

✓ **Make the CEO your chief recruiter**—Top CEOs understand the value of star performers, and they personally make recruiting top talent a priority. CEO's must act as role models and send the message to everyone that they are the chief recruiter for the organization. Senior officers must attend recruiting events and activities and periodically add to their calendar candidate calls and prospect lunches. Have your CEO call superstar candidates. Provide the CEO with information on the candidate, the job and your firm's best selling points.

✓ **Become a retention expert**—Managers must realize that if they don't control retention they will be required to continuously recruit to fill those vacancies. In order to minimize that burden, it's essential that managers become experts in retention. They must spend the time to identify what motivates, excites and frustrates each performer on their team.

✓ **Dedicate some time**—Spend time wooing top talent, or your competition will. Workers have been liberated from your competitors, and the good ones know they are in demand. Visit www.erexchange.com and read about recruiting everyday. Don't limit your learning to the US; it's essential that you also learn how to hire around the globe because global hiring can increase your productivity as well as the quality (performance after hire) of your new employees.

CHAPTER 4

Quit Fishing in the Wrong Places

Chapter 4 Learning Goals:

1. Find out why traditional methods for finding star performers will not work in future. Advertisements are like cattle calls.

2. Understand the value of your time. Spend it wisely by concentrating on the top prospects. The best talent in the market is already working.

3. If you don't know where to find pools of talent that are appropriate, you will waste lots of time fishing in empty waters. Learn where your target candidates can be found, and focus on developing a referral network.

4. When talent nibbles at an opportunity, organizations need to act fast.

"Time is the most valuable thing that a man can spend."
(Theophrastus)

The next morning, my wristwatch alarm went off at six-thirty. In the quiet room, without the usual street traffic outside, the alarm sounded like a smoke detector shrieking in my ear. Surprisingly, however, I felt refreshed. I knew that the break from the city air was probably doing my system some good.

In the next bed, Dale rolled over and looked at me through bleary eyes. His laugh came out like a groan. "What the hell are we doing here, buddy?"

I climbed out of bed and dialed Sue-Lee's room. Dale and I had been college roommates, so sharing a room together was quite natural. Sue-Lee was in a room to herself next door, although now, because she wasn't picking up her telephone, I was starting to wonder if she had made a break for it in the middle of the night. Finally, I heard her groggy voice say hello.

"Time to wake up, Princess," I said.

There was silence for a moment before she spoke. "Pete, I'm not sure about any of this. This Hawk guy seems a bit eccentric. I think I just want to head home."

Wondering how serious she was, I tried to gauge how much faith I had in Hawk myself.

"Let's go have breakfast with him … see what he has to say," I replied. "We can always take off mid-morning if it's not going well."

"I guess," she sighed. "What have we got to lose, right?"

* * * * *

We found Hawk frying bacon in the small kitchen of his cottage. His dog was once again sprawled out near the front window. In the morning light, the cottage looked brighter and cleaner than it had in the dark. The built-in bookshelves were jammed with hard covers of all sorts, from blues music to mathematics and physics. Atop Hawk's desk, beside the laptop computer, a wireless modem hummed away, its green blinking lights signaling a connection to the distant world. In a corner of the room in front of a recliner was the small flat-panel television I had seen the night before, and out the side window I caught a glimpse of a satellite dish mounted high on the wall of the cabin. Clearly Hawk wasn't living the reclusive Grizzly Adams life I originally thought he was.

A hallway behind me led presumably to a bedroom and a bathroom, while in front of me the living room opened to a small kitchen nicely equipped with a long wooden countertop, gleaming oak cupboards, and an old fridge and stove. Separating the kitchen and living room was a solid pine table with six heavy chairs around it. The cottage was small yet comfortable, modern yet rustic. I liked it, and I could easily see myself in such a spot once I retired. Unfortunately, I knew that my wife would also easily see me there—all by myself.

We helped ourselves to mugs of coffee from an old metal pot bubbling on the stove. Nobody commented on the black bits floating in their mugs, evidence of the old fashioned method of boiling the grounds directly in the pot on the stove.

"Well, it's not my usual low-fat café mocha," mused Sue-Lee. "But it tastes good, Hawk. Thank you." I noticed that Sue-Lee seemed in good spirits, her tension from the night before all but gone. Evidently a good night's sleep had somewhat softened her impression of P.D. Hawkston. I had to smile. Sue-Lee had always been a good sport back in high school, and I had fond memories of her carefree ways at parties and on ski trips. Like the rest of us, she had since acquired a spouse and kids and a fancy house and a high-stress job, and had grown into what some might call a responsible, upstanding member of society with little time for frivolity—or what others might call 'uptight.' I thought back to Hawk's comment from yesterday that we were sprinting toward retirement, but I suspected that Sue-Lee's finish line would continually move farther and farther away.

Suddenly we heard a light knocking at the back door. Without waiting for Hawk to open the door, a slender middle-aged woman in a yellow sun dress stepped inside the cabin carrying a small jar of something red. "Good morning, everyone, good morning," she beamed, as if she had known us for a long time. "Such a beautiful day. We should be in for another scorcher. I'll have to remember to water my rose bushes before I head into the town."

"Hi, Gladys," Hawk smiled awkwardly, his head ducking slightly. His body language said it all. He seemed slightly embarrassed, like a teenage boy unsure of himself.

"When I was out for my walk this morning," the woman said, gently patting Hawk's arm, "I noticed the strange car in your driveway, and I thought you could use some of my homemade raspberry jam for your breakfast guests." She set the jar on the counter.

"That's very thoughtful of you," said Sue-Lee, who stepped forward to introduce herself. When introductions were made all around, there followed a moment of silence where nobody knew what to say.

"Well ... I have to run along, I guess," said Gladys, who clearly looked like she did *not* have to run along, and wanted nothing more than to sit and learn more about her neighbor's houseguests. "The pottery shop opens at nine, and I want to pick up something for my granddaughter's birthday." She started toward the door. "Hawk, my dear, will we be seeing you at the bridge tournament Sunday night?"

Hawk turned red and quickly swiveled back toward the stove where he began heating a second frying pan. "Umm, I'm not sure. Probably."

"Excellent," she said, then turned to us. "He's a whiz with numbers. He seems to be the only one who knows that raising a bid of two or three no-trump to four no-trump should be quantitative, not Blackwood."

"Oh, sure," I said, blinking. "I have that problem all the time."

Gladys said goodbye. As soon as the door closed behind her, Dale sang out to Hawk. "She *li-ikes* you. She's yer gurrrrlfriend."

"Nonsense," he scowled, as if Dale were being a little too familiar. "She's a friend. We play cards together. That's it."

"Have you asked her out on a date?" asked Sue-Lee.

"Don't be silly. Men my age don't *date*."

We had a few more laughs at our host's expense, but he wasn't biting.

"So what's our test for today?" I finally asked, buoyed by the fact that our invincible headhunter was a little more human than we had thought.

A bowl full of pre-sliced bell peppers and mushrooms emerged from the fridge, and Hawk melted some butter in the second frying pan. "Your first test is this: I want you each to go into town this morning and recruit some whippersnappers to come out here and do some odd jobs. I've got all kinds of yard work to do."

He saw three high-level businesspeople look at one another and then stare back at him. He obviously sensed our mood. "What's the matter?"

Dale spoke up. "*That's* the test? You want *us* to find your grunt labor for you?"

"In so many words, yes. And there are ten points on the line for each person you recruit."

"No offense," I said, "but I don't think we came all the way out here for this."

"What did you come out here for, Peter?"

"To learn how to 'win talent.' That's the phrase that we keep hearing."

Hawk flipped the diced vegetables into the pan where they immediately started hissing and spitting. "You *will* learn."

"Look. We're busy people," said Sue-Lee. "With all due respect, we'd rather just get a few key tips on recruiting from you."

Hawk still had his back to us. He began cracking eggs into a bowl on the counter. "You all know where the door is, then. No charge for what we talked about so far."

Again, we stared at each other, not knowing what to say. Finally, Dale stood up and walked over to the stove for more coffee. "I've been going to training seminars and conferences for twenty-five years and nobody has ever told me to do anything as ridiculous as this to learn." His face broke into a smile. "I like it. I'm in."

True to his word, Hawk's omelet was superb, served with crispy bacon, fried potatoes and thick slices of whole grain toast. We washed it down with orange juice and more hot coffee. When we were full, Hawk told us to eat some more. "You're going to need it," he said with a gleam in his eye.

* * * * *

We returned from our excursion into town three hours later, our first test behind us. The late morning sun was already baking my shoulders as I sat on the dock in front of the cabin and soaked my sore feet in the cool water of the lake. Dale, who had stripped down to his underwear and had jumped right in, was now floating on his back. Sue-Lee had tried retreating to the sofa in the cabin for a rest, only to have the stifling, non air-conditioned heat chase her back outside where she now sat in the shade on the cabin deck.

"Where is Hawk? I'm starving," said Dale, who was perpetually hungry.

"I could use a bite, too," I said. Hawk wasn't around, and I had thought about searching through his refrigerator for a snack, but decided I'd give it another fifteen minutes to see if he turned up.

As if on cue, we suddenly heard the sound of an oar on water and Hawk rounded the bend in a weather-beaten canoe. Scraps sat in front, his head slumped over the edge and his eyes closed, as if he were a passenger on the most boring voyage ever.

Hawk pulled up beside the dock, a portable AM radio beside him buzzing news courtesy of NPR radio. I could see a folded *New York Times* newspaper lying beside him on the bench. An empty Krispy Kreme Donuts paper cup lay discarded in the bottom of the boat beside a large unopened tub of Kentucky Fried Chicken. He pulled out several cold beers from a cooler in the bottom of the canoe and tossed one each to Dale and me. We thanked him profusely as we drained half of it right away. Sue-Lee must have heard us, and her high school beer drinking past couldn't keep her away from the dock. "Thank you," she said, as she walked out onto the dock and accepted a beer from Hawk, who was now standing on the dock with his hands on his hips.

"What happened to you guys?" he said, lifting the edge of his wide-brimmed hat. "You look like you've been dragged through the desert behind a horse."

"It was useless," Sue-Lee sighed.

"A waste of time," I grunted.

"There are no damn teenagers in that town," Dale said. "We looked everywhere."

"No teenagers," repeated Hawk thoughtfully. "Hmm … where did you look?"

"I tell you," continued Dale, "we walked up and down that scorching main street fifty times. There was an arcade and an ice cream store, but no kids hanging around."

"I see," said Hawk. He stepped out onto the dock and tied the canoe's rope around a post. He stood a moment and stared out across the lake. Then he shrugged. "Oh well, no points for any of you." He reached down and grabbed some fishing rods and a tackle box from the canoe. "Let's go fishing."

"What?" said Sue-Lee. "That's it?! 'Let's go fishing'?"

"Yep. Come on. Ten points on the line for whoever catches the first fish." He whistled at his dog, who turned to watch him for a moment, then seemed to sigh as if he were being asked to do a huge favor—or learn a complex new trick. Finally, the dog stood, stretched, then lazily crawled up out of the canoe and followed his master along the shoreline to a shady spot on the bank.

A half hour later, plump and full from the Kentucky Fried Chicken, the four of us sat on a shaded escarpment above a small tributary in the lake, away from the noise of the speedboats and jet skis near the beach around the bend. A burbling creek flowed into the lake about a hundred yards from where we sat, and several seagulls floated listlessly overhead. The scent of pine and wildflowers drifted lazily around us. I wasn't sure which I was more thankful for: the shade, the light breeze off the lake, the chicken, or the cold beer that Hawk had mercifully provided. At any rate, we were in much better spirits as we sat lined up with our fishing rods pointing out over the water. Unfortunately, we had been sitting there for fifteen minutes and the only thing that had dipped was Dale, in the lake in his underwear again.

"You can be such a pig," laughed Sue-Lee when he emerged from the water, his black boxer shorts clinging to his pudgy white thighs. It was the first time I had heard Sue-Lee laugh in weeks.

Determined to win ten points for catching the first fish, I kept a close eye on the small red and white bobbers floating in the water about twenty yards in front of us. Hawk had given us instructions to yank the line and reel like crazy if the bobbers dipped. "The same thing applies to recruiting top talent," he had told us. "When you get a nibble, you can't sit around saying 'I'm too busy. I'll reel it in when I get the chance.' You drop everything and make that your priority. Too many companies say they're committed to the talent principle, but they don't walk the talk."

> Some recruiters have had success looking for people with the right skills (versus merely the right experience) by "narrow casting". This approach suggests for example that you look in rock climbing clubs for risk takers and at former top athletes for those with drive and discipline. One major home hardware firm looks to ex-military officers for leadership and older workers for reliability.

We had been fishing for a half hour when an older gentlemen in hip waders and a fishing hat strolled up and greeted Hawk, who introduced the gentleman as a neighbor.

"How's the fishing?" asked the neighbor, who started chuckling at something.

"Terrible," replied Dale.

"That might be because you're fishing in the wrong place," said the neighbor.

"What?" we all said at the same time.

"There are no fish here," the neighbor answered, turning to point at something. "You see that nice creek feeding into the lake over there? Well, that nice creek flows from town. Not only is it somewhat polluted, it's warm water, and trout don't like warm water … clean or dirty."

Everyone turned to look at Hawk, who just smiled back at us.

When Hawk's neighbor had departed down the path, Sue-Lee cried out to Hawk, "You knew it, didn't you? What the heck are we doing here?"

This brought an apologetic smile to Hawk's face. "I'm sorry. Just a little joke of mine."

"Well, the joke sucks," Dale said.

Hawk responded with the last thing I expected to hear. "How does it feel?" he asked.

Dale snorted. "We wasted our time."

"Kind of like your recruiting efforts today," Hawk said with eyebrows raised. He glanced at his wristwatch then pulled some coins from his pocket and began jingling them in his hand. I could see that they were Kennedy dollars, their silver faces shining in the sun.

As my friends and I sat there, digesting our host's point, Hawk glanced at his watch again and removed a few more Kennedy dollars from his pocket. He now held a small stack of coins in the palm of his hand.

"Okay. I'll bite," Dale said. "What's with the money?"

In 2003, the CEO of an import/export/transportation brokerage company (with offices in every major port city in North America) asked a single question that resulted in the VP of HR being fired on the spot. He had asked which source in use by the company produced the best performing employees. To his dismay, the VP who routinely made requests for increases in budget didn't know the answer. Following the VP's departure, the CEO along with a panel of other executives barraged the remaining HR staff with a list of pointed questions. What emerged from the crossfire was a blueprint for a performance oriented HR function. Less than a week later, the remaining staff had completed the analysis revealing that the firm had been spending the bulk of its resources trying to recruit from sources that had traditionally produced few or no quality hires.

"I thought you'd never ask," smiled Hawk. "I want to touch on the value of time. Regardless of which company department you're in, let's pretend your budget is one million dollars a year. That would mean that your *time* is worth one million dollars per year. Do you know what that works out to on a minute-by-minute basis?"

I looked at the eight coins in his hand and assumed that Hawk was using them as a metaphor. "I'm guessing it's eight dollars."

"That's right. A little more than eight dollars a minute. Almost five-hundred dollars per hour. Think about the amount of time you've just wasted here fishing and figure out the opportunity cost of that time."

Hawk let that sink in, before continuing. "Now, can you really afford to be wasting your five-hundred dollar per hour time?"

We had to admit that we couldn't.

"So ... if you don't know where to fish, you'll waste a whole lot of time casting your line in the wrong places."

"Like walking up and down Main Street," I said.

"Precisely," said Hawk, as we all began packing up. "That may generate some good candidates, but it's not likely. It's not targeted enough. It's like placing an ad in the newspaper. How many great people do you really think apply on those ads?"

"I have the feeling you're going to tell us it's not many," said Dale.

"Less than fifteen out of a hundred successful new hires are ever generated from a newspaper ad," responded Hawk. "That means it's 85% *in*effective."

"Why so poor?" I asked.

"Think about yourself. Have you *ever* applied to an ad in the paper?"

I had never really thought about it. "No," I answered. "I guess I've always gotten my jobs through contacts I know. Or the company came calling directly and wooed me into leaving. Anyway, I'm not actively looking for another job, so why would I look at job ads? Plus there are so many ads to read, I just wouldn't have the time."

"And what if you did accidentally come across an advertised position that looked like a terrific fit for you, would you apply?"

"Probably not."

"Why?"

"Confidentiality concerns would make me reluctant. Resumes always end up stuck in a pile in the HR department, or on the desk of some junior person in the hiring manager's department who does the pre-screening. I'd never be certain who was going to see mine. If I were looking to change jobs, I'd want to be extremely cautious and I would want the entire process to be very confidential."

"You're like most star performers," said Hawk. "You're usually not looking for a job and won't even see that newspaper ad. Even if you do happen to see it, you probably won't apply, because you work in a tight-knit industry and you wouldn't want to take the chance of having the word that you are looking get back to your firm, jeopardizing your current position, right?"

> **Successful recruiting is a lot like fishing. If the fish you catch is just floating around, make sure you smell it first.**

"I guess so."

Hawk nodded and started leading us on the path back to the cabin. "Most ads in the newspaper are like cattle calls. The very best people that are currently working just don't read them so what you get are mostly desperate unemployed people and malcontents."

"Okay, I see your point, Hawk," Dale said, as we rounded a bend not far from the cottage. "But where do the other eighty-five percent of new hires come from? Internet job boards?"

Hawk swatted a fly away from his face as he stepped into a clearing. "They're not great either, unless you have highly-specialized positions and need to recruit from a narrow talent pool across the country. A lot of the hype around Monster and Careerbuilder is just that: hype. Monsters can be ugly. There are many problems with large job boards."

"But it seems like a lot of candidates are using them," I pointed out.

"It might seem that way," Hawk grunted. "But did you ever think that the wrong candidates are the ones using these large job boards? In fact, it is rare for large Fortune 500 companies to get more than 10% of their hires from large job boards."

"Why so low?" asked Dale.

"I'll wager that most people don't use it for the same reasons they wouldn't apply to an ad in the paper," said Hawk. "Confidentiality is the one reason, but the bigger one is that the best and the brightest folks are generally working, contributing, producing. They have to be approached and convinced to apply for a job, and job boards just aren't very convincing. If on the other hand, the applicants that you are receiving have a lot of time to talk to you, then you should view them like the restaurant owner who is desperately hawking fliers in front of an empty restaurant, or the dentist hanging out at his reception desk chatting, waiting for a new customer to show up. Don't waste your time on job board candidates. Focus on superior performers who almost invariably are already working. Because these individuals are good at their job, they naturally expect their next 'best opportunity' to come internally from managers at their own firm. So even if they had time, they just don't see the need to look externally on a large, impersonal, electronic job board."

By now we were across the clearing and had almost reached the cabin. Hawk cleared his throat and spoke up again. "So what *is* the most effective recruiting approach? Well, most job placements spring from word of mouth, from the network of contacts that people have. A headhunter's most valuable asset is her Rolodex. Your clients are essentially paying for access to her network of top people. And a great headhunter knows that the most effective use of her time is to work that network and go after good people directly," continued Hawk. "That means headhunting them, or to use an industry term, *sourcing* them. You need to go after the ones who are busy, who aren't rushing to return your calls. Just like a hard-to-get restaurant reservation, or tickets to a sold-out show, or an appointment with a renowned medical special-

> During the height of the first War for Talent in the late 1990's, many firms implemented employee referral programs to leverage the eyes and ears of every employee in the recruiting process. While such programs were effective, few firms built them out in such a way to leverage every employee's network. One semiconductor manufacturing firm would routinely jog the memory of employees by asking very specific open-ended questions. The questions got people to recall past contacts that they otherwise would have forgotten or overlooked. It also made the referral program active versus passive. While many firms with referral programs generate, on average, 37% of all hires from employee referrals, this firm routinely generates more than 50% of all hires from referrals.

ist, the best of the best are always in demand. It's the same with talent in the workplace. They're happily employed and rarely respond to ads or even the first call from the headhunter. They feel they don't have to."

"They consider it beneath them?" I asked.

"I guess you could look at it that way. But I suggest you think of it as if they have dozens of opportunities, and you are offering them just one more. Because they are constantly given opportunities within their company, a new one—from an absolute stranger, no less—doesn't seem that exciting. The best and the brightest know they are good, and they know people will come to them with opportunities."

"Sounds like big egos to me," said Sue-Lee.

We stepped up onto the deck and flopped down in the wicker chairs sitting along the wall of the cabin.

"Ego can be good, especially if the ego is built from a string of successes," said Dale. "Some of my top engineers could float a boat with their inflated heads."

"Make no mistake," Hawk replied. "A little ego and self-assuredness is not a bad thing. On the contrary, those are the people I would often go after while sourcing top candidates."

"So, all this talk about placing ads in the newspaper, posting jobs on large Internet boards … we're wasting our money on those things?" asked Dale.

"I didn't say they were a total waste. It could be a good idea to *include* them as a small part of your total recruiting plan, which we'll talk more about later. But my point is that there are much more effective places to go fishing for top talent."

"Okay, expert," said Sue-Lee. "So where should we have been fishing?"

"Over there," said Hawk, motioning with his can of iced tea to a spot on the lake around the bend. "Let's go."

* * * * *

Chapter 4—Manager Action Steps

Some suggested actions for proactive managers include:

✓ **Become a sourcing expert**—It's critical that every manager realizes that *where you look* (or "sourcing") is the most crucial element in recruiting. If you can't find them, you certainly can't convince them to apply. Know what sources produce the best candidates for every job category.

✓ **Stop using techniques from the past**. High unemployment tools and strategies won't work in today's low unemployment economy. Less than 20% of all new hires are generated from a newspaper ad, and a recent poll found that 69% of respondents had never used a job board.

✓ **Focus on the currently employed**—Decide to focus your recruiting primarily on the very best people with up-to-date training and skills. That generally means currently employed top performers. Yes, you must actively "poach" the best away from your competitors. Don't look in newspapers or at career fairs; instead, look across the street in your competitor's building. That's where top performers with up-to-date skills can be found.

✓ **Track the best sources**—Take a look at your most recent hires who turned out to be excellent on-the-job performers and check to see what source was used to find them. Do the same with bottom performers and for jobs where you got few qualified applicants. Once you identify the ineffective sources, reduce your time and spending in those areas (typically newspaper ads, jobs fairs and large job boards). Instead, focus on employee referrals, professional events and name generation activities.

✓ **Rely on referrals**—Realize the importance of networks and referrals in identifying top talent. The number one method for finding star performers is to actively "source" them out.

✓ **Do behavioral profiles**—Identify your own top performers and use them as models to find other top performers. Find out what they read, what events they go to, what organizations they join, etc. Use that profile to source other top performers.

CHAPTER 5

Stop Using the Wrong Bait

Chapter 5 Learning Goals:

1. Be very specific about what type of talent you are going after, so you can locate the right pools and use the right bait. Learn the difference between "active" job seekers and "passive" job seekers, and understand the importance of focusing on the latter.

2. Learn to identify candidates' needs and isolate their job-switching criteria. When trying to attract talent, everyone involved must know what bait will work, and be prepared to use it.

3. Understand that the balance of power has shifted, and top talent now controls the process. Shift how you deal with prospective workers to a "customer" model. Fold your sales processes into your recruitment processes. Realize that, just as you are assessing the talent, they are assessing you, your organization, and your ability to meet or exceed their career expectations.

"The customer is the immediate jewel ... Him we flatter, him we feast, compliment, vote for, and will not contradict."
(Ralph Waldo Emerson)

We moved from the patio to the dock in front of his cabin where Hawk pointed to a small twelve-foot aluminum outboard packed with gear. "Everyone grab a life jacket and hop in." He stepped into the back of the boat by the small Evinrude motor. "Ten points for every fish you catch in a half hour window. And an extra ten points for the biggest fish."

Dale turned to me and grinned. "You might as well just stay behind, Petey. But I'll let you hold my fish when we come back."

"Hah," I retorted. "You couldn't even catch a cold out there."

We all laughed as we carefully got in the boat and took our seats. Within minutes we were humming across the water, the breeze refreshingly cool. As we entered a large bay a half-mile from the main beach, Hawk cut the engine. The only sounds were the lapping of the water on the hull and the distant noise of a jet ski.

Sue-Lee peered over the edge of the boat at the water as if she expected to see a fish staring up at her. She turned to Hawk and said, "You're sure there are fish here?"

"I promise you, there are many fish here," said Hawk, while opening his tackle box. "Here, grab what you like and try your luck."

We stared into the tackle box.

"I'm going for a fake smelt," said Dale, pulling out an artificial fish, silver in color with a shimmering underbelly. He chose the biggest, fattest one of the lot. "You can't go wrong with fake smelts. I once caught a seven pound pike with one of these. With the size of this one, I'll probably snag one twice that size."

Sue-Lee chose a small purple spinner, and I opted for a shiny silver lure—known as a spoon—tied to the end of one of the bobbers I saw sitting in Hawk's tackle box. I didn't know much about fishing, but I did know that trout would often go for spoons.

After our lines were set in the water, we sat back and waited with anticipation, half expecting a flurry of activity. When, after ten minutes, that hadn't happened, we relaxed a bit more.

> A video game manufacturer realized significant increases in recruiting process performance when it stopped shovelling money into advertising that had absolutely no chance of ever reaching the target audience and started funding video game competitions instead. By realizing that video game engineers often played the games themselves, they focused their efforts on the gaming community versus the engineering community to engage a more appropriate audience of potential candidates.

Hawk cleared his throat. "We talked about the value of knowing where to fish, so you're not wasting your time. In a while, you're going to head back into the town and find some hired guns for the yard work at my cottage."

A collective groan went up in the boat.

"So I want to ask you this," said Hawk. "*Where* are you going to be looking for help this afternoon?"

We all looked at one another and shrugged. "There don't seem to be many kids around," I said.

"Did you try the beach?" Hawk said.

"Nope," said Dale. "Those kids are just visiting here on vacation. Why would they take a job for a day or two?"

"You're probably right. Crazy thought," said Hawk. "What about knocking on some of the houses just off Main Street? Asking if they had any kids in the house?"

"We couldn't do that!" I laughed. "That would be like … like invading their privacy or something."

"Plus it would take forever," said Sue-Lee.

"You're probably right again. Silly me."

"So where else?" asked Dale.

Hawk turned to us. "I have just given you two good ideas and, like almost every single person out there trying to recruit staff, you aren't prepared to take those steps. Well, let me tell you, I made a lot of money off of people willing to take short term contracts because that's all they wanted to do. I made even more money off of banging on doors and disturbing the people who everyone else thought didn't want to be disturbed."

"You actually went to their homes?" asked Dale.

"No," said Hawk. "Well, actually, yes, I did do that once, but that's a long story. I'm talking about tracking these people down at their workplace. Or approaching them at trade shows, seminars, or at association meetings, or at health clubs, or wherever."

"But these kids in this town are different," I said.

"Are they?" Hawk said. "Tell me again what you did to recruit your workers today?"

"Like I said, we walked up and down those streets," said Dale. "We even made up some bulletins and posted them on boards and utility poles."

"Let me get this straight again," said Hawk. "You say you three walked up and down that main street fifty times but did not see a *single* teenage boy or girl the entire time?"

Dale shook his head. "No. I said we didn't see any hanging around."

"So you did see some kids?"

"Yes, but that was in the shops."

"What were they doing?"

"Working," answered Dale.

Hawk looked unimpressed. I spoke up to support Dale. "They seemed to have jobs already. In the donut shop, at the gas station, in the souvenir shops, at the bicycle rental stand. Lots were working in the grocery store."

"Did you approach any of them?"

"No," I repeated. "Like I said, they had jobs already."

"I see. They had work already, so why would they want different work, or more work, right?" he said with a touch of sarcasm. "And they certainly wouldn't know other kids and where to find them, would they?"

It struck the three of us at the same moment. We knew exactly where Hawk was going with this and how it related to recruiting within our industries.

"Look," said Sue-Lee. "This is different. This is just a game. With kids, no less. I'm sure if this was the real world, we would have tried harder to recruit them."

"Really? How would you have tried harder to recruit them?" asked Hawk.

"I don't know. We just would have."

"Okay. You've got a chance to prove it." Hawk said. "This afternoon you can redeem yourselves and earn some points."

Approaching someone you don't know can be daunting for the average person, but one municipality found that most employees were afraid to approach others about coming to work for the city because they didn't know what to say. In response, the city conducted surveys and focus groups to identify what aspects of working for the city current employees found most attractive. Then they asked potential candidates to prioritize the points the employees had identified. With a firm understanding of what was attractive about working for the city, leaders set out to arm all employees with interesting stories they could share that touched on each of the selling points.

"Right on," said Dale, jabbing his finger at me. "You're going down, chump!"

"In your dreams," I laughed.

"Tell me," Hawk said, "what kind of bait are you going to be using this afternoon?"

We all shrugged, and then Dale pointed at the tackle box. "Big, fat juicy smelts?" he said.

Hawk frowned. "What kind of bait were you using in town this morning when you were trying to snag the elusive teenagers?"

Sue-Lee and Dale looked at one another. Dale spoke up. "We created a bulletin and handed it out to a few people. We thought it would make the job look more official."

"You guys were working together?" I cried.

"Just on creating the bulletin," Sue-Lee said, somewhat apologetically. "And really it was nothing. I just scribbled on a piece of paper and then we made some photocopies at the drug store."

"What did your bulletin say?" asked Hawk.

"Just what you'd expect: '*Part time job this weekend only. Great pay.*' The usual."

"Ahh," Hawk said knowingly. "I can see we're going to have to spend some time on how to write enticing material. We'll cover that later. For now, you need to focus on how you'll identify or get referrals to potential hires. When you head into town, I want you to go into some of those stores and approach people who are already working. I also want you to walk up to at least three houses and knock on the door. Whoever you talk to, whether it's in a store or at a house, tell them about the job, and then ask the question, '*Who do you know who could handle the job?*' And note that it's an open-ended question. Whenever you ask the closed question "*Do you know anyone who'd be interested?*" people invariably say they don't know anybody, but they'll keep it in mind. You have to ask them *Who* they know. Never mind if you think those referrals will be interested or not. Once you've found them, then you can start the next critical recruiting step,

> One US bank involves every employee in its "recruiting culture" and as a result, 56% of its hires come from employee referrals … and they have no formal referral program or bonus for making referrals.

determining what it would take to get them interested in accepting the job."

Sue-Lee nodded, paying careful attention. "So we not only need to look in the right places, but we need to know *how* to entice others to help us," I said.

"Right. So when we get back, that's your challenge. There are ten points on the line for every person you recruit."

"When are we going to get to actually start developing our recruiting strategy?" Sue-Lee asked.

Hawk gazed out at the water like he had all the time in the world. "We'll get there."

We sat for another fifteen minutes, but the water lay still around us with no sign of fish below. Just then, Hawk's fishing buddy neighbor came along in a boat of his own, trailing a line in the water behind him.

"Any luck?" he called out after pulling up beside us and shutting off his motor.

"Rotten," said Hawk. "Reel in your lines, everybody."

We did so, and my red and white bobber swam toward me. When we all had our lines out of the water, we heard laughter from the other boat. "Just as I thought. You're fooling with your guests again, Hawk," said the neighbor. "That's why I followed you out here."

Hawk grinned as if to say, *What, me?*

"I don't get it. What's so funny?" Dale asked.

The older gentleman leaned toward us. "You," he said to Dale. "You've got a smelt on there that could choke a bear. You won't catch anything in this lake with a smelt that big."

"Pardon me?" Dale replied.

"Same with your silver spoon," he said to me. "You have to be casting and reeling. It can't just sit there under a bobber. You need worms if you want to use a bobber. And you," he said, pointing to Sue-Lee. "You've got a spinner on, but you're not trolling. You can't just throw a spinner out and have it motionless."

We all turned to Hawk, who simply smiled and started packing everything up. The neighbor was still chuckling as he started his engine again and headed off.

"Real funny," Dale said. "You did it again. You knew we weren't going to catch anything."

"You chose the bait, not me," smirked Hawk. "All we've talked about so far is *where* to fish, not which bait to use."

"So why didn't you tell us?" said a perturbed Sue-Lee.

"You didn't ask."

She sighed. "So, what *is* the right bait?"

"Well, before I answer that," said Hawk, scratching his chin. "Let me ask you what kind of fish you're trying to catch?"

Sue-Lee shrugged. "I don't know. Whatever's down there."

"You said there's trout in the lake," I said.

"What kind of trout?" asked Hawk. "There are several species in here."

"I was going after pike, myself," said Dale.

"That's great," said Hawk. "But you had no idea what size the pike are in this lake and whether or not they could manage a large lure like you had on."

"So we should have asked you which bait to use?"

"Before that, you should have decided which fish you were going after. In business terms, you have to define your target market before you put a product out there."

"Oh, for goodness sake," said Sue-Lee. "Now we're talking about the fish being the customer?"

Hawk offered a Buddha-like smile. "It's a great metaphor, isn't it?"

An international restaurant chain surveys a random sample of its employees and a targeted group of candidates each year to determine what is most important to them in selecting or staying with an employer. The survey then goes on to ask existing employees how the firm rates against other firms they have previously worked for. This information is heavily relied upon to determine which programs and work environment characteristics to keep constant, and which to change.

"Look, I know exactly what kind of staff I need to hire," said Sue-Lee. "Our company has defined job profiles, and we know ahead of time what we want."

Hawk cocked his head sideways. "Listen to what you just said. You used the pronouns 'I,' 'our,' and 'we.' Those are all company focused. What if McDonalds just churned out hamburgers because their chairman of the board liked the taste of them?"

"Okay, so we need to focus more on the target market," I said, somewhat grumpily.

"In the new economy, yes, that's what I'm saying. Sticking an ad in the newspaper or on the Internet is like you blindly throwing a fishing line in the water and then sitting in your boat, hoping someone out there bites. It's not targeted enough."

"And the target is the candidate?" I added.

"Yes. Hiring managers can no longer just dangle something shiny in front of the top potential applicants because, as we saw before, they are probably not even looking. But even candidates who have expressed an interest won't always take the bait. With most companies, that shiny bait is money. They simply throw more dollars in front of a prospective hire and think that'll do it. Sometimes it will. But with the top talent, it's not about money."

Hawk paused and I sensed that he was waiting for us to ask him exactly what this was all about. Instead, the three of us sat sulking while he revved up the motor and turned us toward the cottage. On the way back across the water, we sat staring out at the distance, trying to suppress our annoyance with Hawk.

Finally our host broke the silence. "So, we've already agreed that we have to know *where* to fish. And now we agree we have to know *what* to fish with. We have to give 'em what they're looking for," Hawk called out over the noise of the motor. "We, as managers, can think it's the greatest job or greatest compensation package in the world, but if your target doesn't think so, you're not going to catch him. Just like when trying to land a new paying customer, you better have done some research on your candidates, have done a thorough needs assessment, and found out what they require in order to make a move."

"A needs assessment on candidates?" said Sue-Lee, raising her voice in exasperation. "Look, this is how we recruit at our firm: we interview someone, tell them about a position, do our best to convince them to take it, and that's it. Either they want the job or they don't."

"And are you still catching them that way?" Hawk asked, his eyebrows raised.

No answer was needed. Sue-Lee lowered her eyes, sat back, and folded her arms across her chest.

"The recruiting landscape is changing," said Hawk as he carefully watched a larger speedboat cutting directly across our path. I could see the wake from the speedboat and knew we'd hit some larger waves within half a minute. He said, "It's absolutely imperative that you start looking at it from a sales and marketing angle, with the talent being the customer. That's one of the most important things you'll learn today. Recruiting is a form of sales and many of the same principles and approaches must be applied to recruiting."

"I don't like all this talk about selling," said Sue-Lee. "I'm not a sales person."

"Sue-Lee, business is all *about* selling," Hawk said. "There is a sales component to *every* business function out there. If a company has no customers, it won't survive. That's an immutable law in business. Every single company has to have salespeople to find the customers."

"We don't have salespeople at our CPA firm," Sue-Lee said.

"Yes, you do. You're one of them."

"No, I'm not," she said indignantly, with her hands facing out, almost as if she were pushing away the very title itself. Our boat had slipped up one side of a larger wave and now crashed down on the other side. We had to grab both sides of the boat to steady ourselves. "I'm a *partner* in a professional firm," she shouted over the noise. "I'm sorry, but I didn't work for twenty years as a CPA to be called a salesperson."

Hawk sat forward for a moment and studied the waves. He positioned the boat to reduce the impact of the next wave. "You're getting hung up on the title. What I'm talking about is the process. In your job, you have sales-related activities, don't you? Only you use the euphemism *business development*, am I right?"

She nodded. "Business development is part of what I do."

"Sure it is," said Hawk. "It's your job to schmooze clients, take them to lunch, take them golfing. You're always networking with CFOs and controllers of companies in hopes of winning their audit and tax business, right? And if you do win new clients often enough, then people at the firm would say you're good at business development."

"I still don't like it," said Sue-Lee, her arms folded across her chest.

I was getting a bit impatient with her and decided to speak up. "The act of selling isn't inherently bad, Sue-Lee. We're all sales people. Sales is about convincing someone else to adopt your point of view. We do it every day, at home with our kids when we're trying to get them to do their homework or eat their vegetables. We do it with our spouses when we're debating which movie to see. We do it with our bosses when asking for raises or with subordinates when asking them to work late to finish a project."

"And tell us, who are the best salespeople in the entire world?" grinned Hawk.

"Kids," I replied quickly. "Children are the best salespeople in the world. They're gunslingers when it comes to using emotion. They have no shame or embarrassment about pleading, cajoling, whining. I've seen your girls, Sue-Lee. They whip out those pretty eyes and toothy grins and you can't say no."

I watched her sigh and throw up her hands. "Fine. I'll try to change my old way of thinking. Selling is okay."

Hawk began easing the boat around the bend toward the shallow, still cove near his property. We were only fifty yards away from land when he finally cut the engine and pulled it out of the water on its hinge, just as the boat bumped gently up against the dock. Dale grabbed a post and steadied the boat while Sue-Lee began climbing out.

"In the new war for talent, what's the problem with that old approach, one where you just focus on checking off your own requirements like a shopping list?"

During the high-tech boom of the late 1990's one manufacturer of scientific instruments was so interested in pre-identifying what candidates were interested in that it created a process that asked candidates to develop their own dream job description. The information was then used to create a tailored candidate assessment that helped both parties answer questions about the other and demonstrated that the firm would be capable of making the dream job more of a reality than any other firm could.

Sue-Lee said, "It's not a customer-driven process."

"Right," nodded Hawk. "These days, candidates have their own shopping lists and their own requirements to tick off. The candidate is waiting for you to deliver on *their* needs. For example: more challenge and learning—check! Flexible hours—check! An office with a window—check! If you spend the whole time staring down at your own list when you should be looking over at theirs, you won't know which requirements they are waiting for you to call out. Rather than the typical one-sided approach, you need instead to listen to the candidates, to engage them, to find out what kind of people they are, to identify what they really want to achieve during their careers. You won't find that information by staring down at a job description. Or even by looking at their resumes."

Sue-Lee sighed. "So we're back to this thing about the candidate being the customer?"

"Absolutely," cried Hawk. "There is no more important point today than that. You are not holding the cards any longer. The power has shifted to the candidate."

"That's a little frightening," I said. "It used to be that people felt lucky to have a job."

"It's a huge shift," agreed Hawk, as he continued to unload the boat.

We heard Dale sigh. "I know I'll have a hard time changing. We used to just stick an ad in the paper and get flooded with applicants. Whoever we made an offer to almost always accepted."

"Why do you think that was true?" asked Hawk.

"Because they needed a job."

Hawk let the words sink in. After he moment he said, "They needed *a* job, didn't they? Not the perfect job, but *a* job. And now everything is changing due to talent and skill shortages. Now some people might still fit into that 'need-a-job' category, but if you're not extremely careful, you'll drive away the very best candidates with your self focus, and the only remaining candidates will be these *need-a-job* people. Actually, the worst thing that could happen is that these *need-a-job* types will actually jump at your offer, which would mean you would lose your chance to get a top-performing employee, while simultaneously being saddled with someone who is likely to be below average. That's the learning here: people with below average skills will jump at opportunities, while the most desirable people have to be courted and listened to. Once again, the very best people are not looking for *a* job, but they're looking for *the* job. The *right* job. And the most qualified can afford to be choosy. Headhunters understand that. If you don't understand that and set your pride aside, then you're going to fail in your effort to recruit top candidates."

I thought hard about what Hawk was saying, and suddenly I remembered a bestselling business book I had recently read called *Who Moved*

My Cheese? by Spencer Johnson and Ken Blanchard. I briefly told the others about it, then concluded by saying, "So the bottom line with the book is we have to adapt to change. When it comes to hiring people, we can't keep expecting an abundance of candidates to be there when we need them, because they won't be."

"Great example, thanks," said Hawk. "Griping about a situation that has changed won't change it back."

"It still seems backward," grunted Dale. "I guess I'm old-school enough to think that people should view a job as a privilege, not a right."

Hawk grinned. "That's the nut of it, right there. Employees will be scarce, so they'll hold more power. In fact, the balance of power is changing like you would not believe."

"And the leaders who understand that you must now treat talent like customers will attract the best talent and, as a result, they will win," said Sue-Lee slowly.

"That's right," Hawk said, as we stretched on the dock. The afternoon sun felt warm on my skin, and I inhaled the fresh breeze swirling around me.

"I still don't like it," grumbled Dale. "I'm the one who built the company up. I have a lot of pride in that, and I don't think my pride is standing in the way. I think it makes me a better manager, quite frankly."

"I'm sure it does," Hawk said.

"But back there you just said to get rid of my pride."

"No, I said to set your pride aside when you're recruiting new hires. Try being more humble and lose the 'my way or the highway' mindset."

"I've been working on that," grinned Dale. "Cuz it's like Ted Turner said: 'If I just had humility, I'd be perfect.'"

We laughed, but none harder than Dale himself.

"So we're supposed to be chummy with candidates?" Sue-Lee said. "Act like they're going to be an instant partner in the firm, or something?"

"No, they're still going to be working for you. You still have to be very clear on roles, responsibilities and reporting structure."

"Still ... I don't know," she replied. "We've been very successful doing things our way all these years. I don't want the staff to start thinking they can run the show."

Hawk sighed. "You've probably heard of the author Robin Sharma. In his book *The Greatness Guide*, he writes that nothing fails like success. People become arrogant and rest on their laurels. Sharma said, 'The more successful you and your organization become, the more humble and devoted to your customers you need to be.'"

"And in this case our talent is the customer," I said.

"Right," answered Hawk, as he let the point sink in. Then he stood and motioned us toward the cabin. "Now, everyone go wash up. We're heading into town."

* * * * *

Chapter 5—Manager Action Steps

Some suggested actions for proactive managers include:

- ✓ **Identify *their* needs**—In addition to developing a process to identify the best places to look for candidates, it is equally important to identify their "job switching" criteria. With top talent, it's not about the money. Do your research on the candidate—a needs assessment—and find out what they need in order to make a move.

- ✓ **View candidates as "customers"**—Employers are not holding the cards any longer. The old days, when employees were "lucky to have a job", are gone. Realize that top talent does not fit into the "need a job" category. Great people aren't looking for *a* job; they're looking for *the* job.

- ✓ **Shift to a customer-service model**—Traditional recruiting processes have focused on the needs of the company or the requirements for the job. As talent shortages increase (and the candidate's power increases) you must shift attitude and procedures to ensure that the candidate is central to the process. Just as you would with a prospective new customer, eliminate all "frustrators" for candidates so that they don't prematurely drop out of the process.

- ✓ **Recruiting is Sales, with a crummy budget**—Teach your managers to think of recruiting as a *sales* process. Show them how to identify top prospects, qualify them, market to them, "close" the sale and then reinforce the sale after the offer is accepted. Realize that because these targeted candidates have so many opportunities, it takes a high level of sales skills to get them interested. Work with the marketing and sales department in order to identify market research and sales techniques you can use to identify candidate needs.

- ✓ **Develop your network**—Develop a contact list of people who will refer you to top performers. Focus on identifying the best referrals, because it is the single most important thing you can do to improve the quality (ie. on-the-job performance) of hires. Source a network of targeted people and go after top talent directly. Most job placements of star performers come from word of mouth or cold calling to ask "Who's the best?" Also make sure that individuals who benchmark in search of best practices at other firms don't just identify best practices but also identify the best talent in each key best practice area.

✓ **Use your existing staff**—Go directly to your own top performers and ask them to provide the names of the best colleagues they have worked with in the past. Ask them, "Who do you know who could handle this job?" Don't allow your employees to attend conferences or events without returning with the names of the best people they met. Teach your managers and employees to ask open-ended questions that identify people who they *know* can handle the job. Asking the right questions will yield more and better referrals.

CHAPTER 6

How Do They Take Their Coffee?

Chapter 6 Learning Goals:

1. Learn practical questions for uncovering candidate needs. If you truly want top performers, you have to realize that they can afford to demand more from their wish list when it comes to a job.

2. Landing star talent will require managers and organizations to be more flexible in job design.

3. Learn to qualify and pre-close your "customers," without overselling. Nothing can damage an organization more than attracting talent with a pitch you have no intention or capability to deliver.

> *"Find a job you love and you'll*
> *never have to work a day in your life."*
> **(Confucius)**

The main street of the town was as long as a football field and culminated at the beach on the north end. Lining the avenue were quaint shops with impossibly cute false fronts to please the tourists. I saw BMWs and Land Rovers parked up and down the street, with their Tommy Hilfiger owners and Gap kids wandering up and down the sidewalks licking ice-cream cones while attempting to soothe their sunburned bodies.

"Now remember," said Hawk, as he pulled up to a shady curb, "the prospective hire must now be viewed like a prospective customer. With a customer, you'd do what it takes to win that business, which would include identifying their 'buying criteria' right?"

We all nodded.

"And in hiring, you're going to have to do what it takes to win that talent. You'll have to set your pride aside when hiring. Remember, the candidate is the customer and you have to identify their new job and new company 'buying criteria' also."

"And the customer is king," I pointed out.

"Absolutely," Hawk said, motioning to the main street. "Now off you go to find some go-getters for my yard work. I'll meet you back here in ninety minutes."

"An hour and a half? That's it?" I said.

He laughed. "Hey, for the best headhunters, that's more than enough time. Let's get going!" he said, clapping his hands together as if he had just quarterbacked a play in the huddle.

Following orders, we split up and each headed into different stores to try recruiting. I was surprised at how uneasy I was as I wandered through the produce section of the small supermarket and approached a couple of teens unpacking tomatoes from a box.

"Hi, guys," I said, trying to sound both nonchalant and hip at the same time. I almost threw in a quick *WhazzUp?*, but thought better of it.

"Howzitgoin," said the taller of the two, whose name tag read Dru. It was either that or he was a budding rapper named Dr. U honing his skills with hothouse tomatoes in the local Super Food Mart. He looked at me, but he didn't offer any assistance, something my mother would have pointed out was the problem with kids today. No sense of courtesy or respect.

"Look, I'm, uh … I'm trying to hire some kids to do some work at one of the cabins near here. Do you know anyone who might be interested?"

"Not that I know of," said Dru.

"Do you know anyone?" I asked the other teen. "I could really use some help."

The kid shrugged and looked at his taller co-worker, as if the answer was written on Dru's face.

I thanked them and wandered away, realizing that I had completely forgotten Hawk's advice. I had asked them a '*Do you know anyone?*' closed question instead of '*Who do you know?*', and I had forgotten to add the words '*... who could handle that job.*'

Down a tinned goods aisle I found a blonde girl manually sticking price tags on cans of evaporated milk. Apparently bar code technology hadn't infiltrated cottage country yet.

When I asked the proper question this time, I saw the same shrug, but at least she had the inquisitiveness to ask what type of odd jobs they were.

"I'm not sure," I said. "Just some stuff around the house." I immediately realized by the look in her eyes that creepy vagueness was not the right answer. "I mean, it would be yard work. I think there'd be some painting, maybe some lawn mowing, who knows—maybe some gardening." Suddenly I was blathering. "It would pay well. And there's a little secluded beach there for cooling off after, and ..."

Suddenly she was walking away from me, quickly, looking back every step or two to make sure that I wasn't following her, as she no doubt made her way to the manager to report a pervert trying to pick up sixteen year-old girls in aisle three.

I left the grocery store in a hurry and walked halfway up Main Street before turning back to see if anybody was chasing after me. I was angry with myself for the way I had handled things. I realized that I didn't even know exactly what the job entailed, an oversight that I knew P.D. Hawkstone had set us up for. He didn't tell us, because we didn't ask. We thought "yard work" was all we needed to know. That would have been like me trying to recruit someone by saying, 'I have a computer programming job for you. Not sure what kind of programming it is, exactly, but do you want it?' We should have asked Hawk more details. We should have known the job description, and the things that made the job interesting, inside out.

I wiped my brow. A sign in the window beside me said "Jolly's Video," so I stepped quickly inside.

"Hey," came the greeting from a bored young woman of about twenty standing behind the counter. She had a warm enthusiastic grin, and I liked her immediately. After explaining—in fabricated detail—what type of work I had available, the clerk nodded her head and smiled.

"Be tough to find anyone around here for that," she chirped. "Half the stores in town have *Help Wanted* signs in the window. My dad can't even find an evening shift worker for when I go back to college in the fall."

I thought about Hawk's lecture. "Who do you know who could handle that kind of work?" I said, proud of my recovery. In a strange way, this little game had gotten hold of me, and I wanted badly to beat Dale.

She squinted in thought. "Well, you could try this guy I know named Tommy. He comes and stays here every summer with his grandparents. He's not working. In fact he doesn't do too much except skateboard." She pointed behind me to a tree-lined street two blocks away from the beach. She didn't know the house number, but she told me it was the third house from the end on the right side, a white bungalow with blue trim.

A few minutes later, I was standing in front of the house. A fresh coat of paint had been recently applied to the homemade mailbox out front. The mailbox had a name on it: *Stevenson*. The front yard, neatly kept and erupting in color from the dozens of flowers planted there, had the look of a small botanic garden.

"Can I help you?" came a voice to the right. An elderly lady stepped out from behind a hedge and smiled at me.

"Oh, excuse me," I said. "I was told I could find a young fellow named Tommy here. We may have some part time work for him, if he's interested. Over at one of the cottages around the bend."

"Which cottage?"

"A fellow with the last name Hawkston," I said, suddenly realizing I didn't know what the initials in P.D. Hawkston stood for.

"Oh, Hawk," she said warmly. "What a nice gentleman. You tell him I said hello."

"I will, thanks. But do you think Tommy would be interested in the work?"

The woman laughed softly. "Work? You could ask him, but I doubt it. He usually comes up here to relax and do nothing for the summer."

I was about to thank her and turn away, when I suddenly thought of Hawk shaking his head and scolding me for not being more persistent. "May I talk to him for a minute?"

Several minutes later, Tommy's grandmother had extracted him from in front of the TV and was leading him out the front door of the bungalow toward me. He was a tall, gangly teenager with an overgrown hedge of brown hair and a slouched walk. His pants hung loosely around his hips in that style my own kids adored—a style that I hated.

"Hi, my name is Peter," I said when he stood before me, his eyes sporadically darting up to make eye contact with me. "I'm looking to hire someone for some yard work for a day or two. Do you think you'd be interested?"

Tommy shrugged and squinted at me. "I don't know. What kind of stuff you need done?"

"Some painting, pruning trees, fixing up the dock," I said. My fabricated job description was getting better and better by the minute.

"What's it pay?"

I suddenly realized that I didn't know. "Eight dollars an hour," I said, flying by the seat of my pants.

There wasn't even a glimmer of excitement in the kid's eyes. In fact, I thought I saw the corner of his mouth curl up slightly, as if to say, *That's it?"*

"Look, I don't really know what teens around here are making, so if it has to be higher—I don't know, nine or ten bucks an hour—then so be it." I wasn't about to lose this hot prospect and had decided that even if my figure was more than what Hawk wanted to pay then I'd cover the difference myself.

"I'm not sure. Maybe. I'll think about it," Tommy mumbled.

"Okay, I'll give you my cell phone number," I said, reaching for one of my business cards in my wallet and handing it to him. He nodded and then turned back toward the house. I made small talk with the grandmother for a few more minutes then excused myself.

I headed off down the street, recognizing a disappointed feeling within me, wondering if my competitors had rounded up some workers. Suddenly it struck me how wrapped up in this silly little game I had become, and I had to laugh at myself. I decided to knock on a couple more doors, just as we had promised Hawk we would. No further luck. Both houses were occupied by mature residents in their sixties, friendly folks who, after an explanation of what I was up to, told me to pass along their regards to Hawk, but, gosh golly were *darned* if they knew any kids who were available.

My second recruiting attempt had also ended in failure.

Back at the meeting spot I saw Sue-Lee and Dale, and there beside them stood two fresh-faced teens, whom they gleefully presented to me like trophies won in battle. One worker each was fewer than they had hoped for, but a number that earned them bragging rights over me.

Hawk warmly greeted the two teenagers Sue-Lee and Dale had recruited. He told us to grab an ice cream or something while he drove the kids over to his cottage and set them to work on raking leaves, mowing the lawn, and trimming tree branches near the cottage. "When I'm back in half an hour," Hawk said, "it'll be time for your next lesson."

* * * * *

We followed Hawk across main street and entered one of those specialty coffee shops with the overstuffed chairs and soft jazz music which the yuppies had brought with them from the city. I felt right at home, and I could tell that Sue-Lee did as well. Coffee houses like this one used to be just big city stuff. Now they were everywhere, from Saratoga, New York, to Lodi, California. There was something oddly comforting and disconcerting about that, all at the same time.

"Peter, do you mind going up to the counter and ordering us some coffee?" Hawk asked.

"Sure," I said.

"Oh, but hang on. When you walk up to the counter, I want you to say the following: 'I'd like four large coffees to go, please.' That's it. That's all you can say—not a single word more. If the girl behind the counter asks you anything, all you can do is repeat the request with the exact words 'I'd like four large coffees to go, please.'"

I shrugged okay, then proceeded toward the counter, behind which stood a smiling young woman with hair tied back in a ponytail. No sooner had I given her my request—using Hawk's exact words—when I realized what was about to happen.

The girl behind the counter said, "What kind of coffee would you like? We have a nice Colombian house blend, a medium Arabica, some lighter flavored coffees like French Vanilla."

I could feel my face turning red. "I'd like four large coffees to go, please," I repeated.

She frowned at me. "What kind, sir?"

I turned around and saw my three comrades sitting at a table nearby. Dale and Sue-Lee were looking out the window at passersby on the street, while Hawk sat grinning at me. Suddenly I became determined to beat Hawk at his own game. I swiveled around again and faced the young woman. Remembering Hawk's admonishment not to *say* anything else, I pointed at the large urn closest to me, something with Sumatra Dark Roast in the title.

"Sure," she said, looking at me strangely. "Should I leave room for cream?"

I nodded. I paid for the coffee, leaving a generous *Forget-I-was-ever-here* tip in the process. Back at the table, I could hear Hawk explaining what had just happened at the counter with me.

"You're lucky Hawk didn't ask you to order lattes," Sue-Lee said. "She would have had a few more questions."

"It's something to see, isn't it?" Hawk said, looking around at the place as if studying it for the first time. "Back in my day, if we wanted a coffee, we went to the diner and some old bird named Alice or Vera would walk over with a pot of coffee and start pouring. You could have it hot or you could have it cold; that was it. Well, the days of the diner are over for most people."

"There are still places like that," Dale said.

"Not many. People have discriminating tastes now, and they can custom order whatever they want. Tall, short, grande, low-fat, non-fat, decaf, sprinkles, syrup … on and on it goes. Heck, I heard that nowadays you can even order coffee made from some special Vietnamese cat turds, and I'm not making that up." He shook his head, as if lamenting the loss of a better time. "The labor market has changed, too. As we now know, top performers aren't looking for *a* job, they're looking for *the* job … just the way they like it. If they want sprinkles on top, someone out there will give it to them."

> Agilent Technologies in 2000 developed a process called "your dream job" which gave the very best applicants a blank sheet of paper and asked them to list the characteristics of their dream job. Most listed job characteristics that were commonly granted at the firm, which made offering them a "personalized" job relatively easy. Money was seldom even the near the top of the requirements on anyone's list.

"So how do we get top talent working for us when they won't look at our jobs?" I asked, thinking about my failed recruiting excursion in town.

"Because you start out wrong. You have a 'job-centric' point of view, whereas you need to start thinking about the other person first. Learn how they take *their* coffee." Hawk stirred some sugar into his cup.

"The candidate is the customer," Sue-Lee said.

Hawk smiled. "Now you're getting it."

"So, if we're treating candidates like customers," said Dale, "how do we sell them on the job? What's the first step?"

Hawk looked at me. "Peter, you're the sales guy. When you're calling on a new client, what do you do?"

"Find out what they need and then educate them about some things they might not be aware of."

"What happens if you start selling right away? What happens if you try pushing Product X on a client when he's really looking for Product Y?"

I winced. "Failed pitch. We have to figure out ahead of time which product the client needs."

"How do you do that?" asked Hawk.

"Ask a lot of questions," I replied.

"What kinds of questions?"

"We ask them things like, *What is your biggest challenge these days? How could your job be easier? What do you like and dislike about your current supplier? Under what circumstances would you do business with us?* Really, all we're doing is identifying the problems the clients have and their decision criteria. And now that I think about it, those same questions would work in recruiting, wouldn't they?"

"Definitely," agreed Hawk.

"But a lot of top talent isn't interested in talking," Sue-Lee reminded us. "We've all tried attracting them. It's not working. We can't catch them."

"Yes, you can," replied Hawk. "A minute ago, Peter provided some questions you could ask. Take one of them and modify it for recruiting."

Dale spoke up. "You could say, '*What do you like and dislike about your current job?*'"

Sue-Lee said, "How about, '*Under what circumstances would you leave your current job?*'"

"Good," replied Hawk. "But that might be a bit threatening, using the term 'leave your current job.' I have a question I have used many times, with great success: '*What would you add or take away if you could magically make your job better?*' That's a nice non-threatening open-ended question—conversational even."

> **Think like a salesperson: A well-trained salesperson will ask you "What do you like and dislike about your current situation? What does the *ideal* situation look like in your mind?"**

He stopped and let the question sink in, before continuing. "Be persistent. There's always something that could be better about their current job—something they'd like to add or something they'd like to get rid of. It's like 'If only this mochaccino didn't have all this gooey topping on it, it'd be perfect.' Or, 'With chocolate sprinkles, this place would become my favorite hangout.' You see, there is a whole list of possible answers as to what makes a job just right. It could be anything. It might be money, but more often it's a chance to do higher level work with new challenges and learning opportunities. So find out what challenges and growth opportunities they want."

"You said a whole list," said Dale. "What else?"

"It could be a different title. Maybe they want to manage more people, or fewer people. Maybe they've always wanted an office, rather than a cubicle. Maybe it's the latest technology, or a chance to work for a great mentor."

"It could be increased vacation," offered Sue-Lee.

"How about more control over their jobs, flex hours, or even part time hours?" I said. "That's becoming a bigger desire for more people."

"Those are some big hot buttons we should keep an ear out for," said Dale.

"Absolutely. Listen hard to what they're saying. Once you've

A study conducted by the Canadian Broadcasting Corporation found that 28% of respondents said their families resented how hard they worked, and 35% said they would take a job with fewer hours for less pay.

done the needs assessment, you're half way there." He turned to me. "Peter, what's the next step in the selling process?"

"After we've heard all their needs," I said, "the next step is to summarize what it is they're looking for. An example might be, 'Mr. Customer, what I'm hearing is that you're not happy with your current widget. It's too big, it's overpriced, and you can't get it in green. Is that correct?' Next, I would ask them if there is *anything else* that's wrong, and 'Are there features you have thought about but aren't sure if they are currently available?'"

"Why do you do that, Peter?" said Hawk.

"It's really simple. We first need to qualify them—to see if there's a realistic chance of meeting their needs and the needs of our firm. We need to identify their decision criteria and predetermine any possible objections and future needs. If we haven't uncovered every single one of their issues, then they could easily back out of the sale later by claiming that there is suddenly something new that doesn't work for them. This step is important in preparation for the next stage."

"And the next stage is …"

"We use *if-then* statements to weed out the tire kickers," I said. "A typical statement would be, 'Mr. Customer, *if* we could deliver to you a widget that is two inches smaller, fifty cents cheaper, and in a green color, *then* do you see any other reason why we can't go ahead with this contract?'"

Hawk turned to Sue-Lee. "Using Peter's technique, what would a typical *if-then* statement be for a hiring manager trying to get a candidate to take a job?"

> A small regional airline with big plans for expansion knew that it needed to hire experienced crew capable of keeping the airline running more efficiently than its competitors but didn't have the money to lure talent away. To remedy the problem, executives added an *if-then* series of questions to the interview process. That enabled them to determine which candidates could be swayed using alternative forms of compensation such as route selection, family passes, and such. Six years later the airline still beats the competition hands-down in efficiency, lending it an operating margin that is hard to argue against.

She thought for a moment, then said, "Mr. Candidate, *if* we provide everything you said you're looking for—a ten-thousand dollar salary increase, four weeks vacation instead of three, and a promotion to regional manager—*then* would you be interested in accepting a job offer?"

"Very good," said Hawk. "Although the word 'interested' is weak. Anyone can say they're motivated and then still get cold feet and back out at the offer stage, claiming they only said they were *interested*. Make sure you keep eliminating tire kickers. Simply say, '*If* we provide everything you said you want, then *will you* accept a job offer?' Top headhunters use language like this. It pre-qualifies the candidate's interest level so you'll know if they're likely to back out or not."

Hawk turned to the group. "Now let me ask you this: Has a salesperson ever sold you something that didn't meet your needs?"

"Sure," said Dale. "Years ago, I bought an old Chevy from a used car lot. It was a piece of crap."

"What did you learn?" asked Hawk.

"That a good salesperson will identify the problem the customer has and then provide a solution," said Dale. "And the solution is one that meets the customer's needs, not the salesperson's."

"And equally important, a good salesperson isn't creating a need; he is just identifying an *existing* need," I said, looking at each of them individually for a moment.

"So how does this relate to recruiting new staff?" asked Hawk.

"You're saying we should first identify their problem,"

At the peak of one of the largest economic expansions to take place in the United States, around 1999, many brokerage firms were struggling to find talent fast enough to keep up with the influx of investment capital available. To attract talent with suitable skills from other industries, many firms embraced radical cultural changes, doing away with the formal dress code, not relying only on graduates from top tier schools, etc. One firm embraced nearly every change possible, at least on the surface. Many new hires realized within a very short period of time that the firm was the same old firm with only a new coat of paint. Over the course of the next three years, a time when most brokerages were on a roll, this firm experienced the industry's highest employee turnover. Major institutional accounts were lost, criminal charges erupted, and the firm's reputation was irrevocably damaged.

exclaimed Dale. "What they're not happy with in their current job. Low pay, unchallenging work, long hours, too much travel ... whatever it might be. It might be a good idea for me to ask every candidate why they left each of their past jobs, right?"

"Sure," agreed Sue-Lee. "Learn what their 'frustraters' were, because this information could be invaluable in ensuring the same issues don't arise again."

"Excellent," beamed Hawk. "What's the next step?"

"Sell them on why they should work for me?" answered Dale.

"Don't forget the middle step," Hawk said. "You first need to assess whether or not your job truly is a good fit, if you really do have a solution that will meet their needs. Remember, I said you have to start thinking of your prospective hire as a customer. If your solution—in other words the job opportunity you're selling—is not what the customer needed, you will have moved that person into your organization and then six months later they will be disenchanted and want to leave. They'll resent you for pulling them away from their old job and overselling them on something that didn't fit with their aspirations. Peter, what happens when you have too many dissatisfied customers on your hands?"

"Word gets out on the street," I answered. "Business goes down. Companies falter."

"The same thing will happen with recruiting," Hawk went on. "People talk within their industry, and word will get out that you're not as desirable a company as people had initially believed. The best headhunters understand this and will never push someone into a job that's not a fit. It's not worth it. It can hurt your external image which companies call their 'employment brand.' Their reputation or brand will suffer and their network of candidates—their lifeline!—will dry up. Besides that, because of guarantees, they'll just have to refill the position after the misled person leaves, which is a waste of their precious time."

"That's why it's so important for us to do our homework and do a thorough needs assessment with potential hires *before* we try to sell them a job. That's what you're saying?" said Sue-Lee.

"Yes," confirmed Hawk. "Just because the candidate is the best doesn't mean they are the best for you. Make sure to find out what their motivation is for considering a new job opportunity."

"So we can put the right bait on the end of the line," Dale said.

"That's right," laughed Hawk. "As I've said, rather than working to make them happy *after* they're in the job, put a little effort in *before* you hire them and make sure they're the type of person who has the best chances of being happy."

"Is there anything else we can be doing?" asked Dale.

"What about asking prospective hires to hang around the office and job shadow for a day?" suggested Hawk. "What about taking them out for a coffee or lunch with some colleagues and letting the candidates see how everyone interacts? Or set up peer interviews so they can get the straight scoop from their future coworkers. Anything that engages them and helps to really find out who they are, how they think and what their work style is like."

"That's pretty obvious," Sue-Lee said. "You don't want someone taking a job they can't handle."

"I'm not talking so much about their technical abilities to do the job. I'm talking more about their style and thinking," replied Hawk. "On paper the person might look good. And the candidate will probably tell you the job is a good fit, because it may *appear* to fill their career need. But a person may get into a job and find it just doesn't fit. She can't articulate why. Often she'll just say it's something about the corporate culture, or that she just didn't click with the boss."

"We hear that all the time in exit interviews," I said. "It's a big problem."

"It's huge," agreed Hawk. "And when it's not a good fit, the new employee often ends up faking it. But we know that when people behave unnaturally for a long period of time they're not happy and effective. One researcher named it Prolonged Adaptive Stress Syndrome, and she says it's everywhere in our business world."

"Anything with 'syndrome' in the title can't be good," snorted Dale.

"What about using personality assessments?" I asked. "That can

> An American researcher named Dr. Katherine Benziger claims that when people try to adapt themselves to fit someone else's expectations, they end up tense and stressed. She says they end up suffering from a condition called Prolonged Adaptive Stress Syndrome, a very common occurrence in today's workplace.

be a good tool for really getting to know someone and determining if it's a good fit or not."

"We already use psychological testing," said Sue-Lee, "but we still have mismatched hires sometimes."

"I don't think you can totally eliminate the problem," Hawk said. "But if you're careful to use only validated and job-related psychological assessments, then you can reduce that risk somewhat. There are hundreds of tests out there on the market. There are the old popular ones such as Myers-Briggs, but I don't recommend them for job assessment purposes. I'd suggest that you consider Hogan, PSI, CPI or Wonderlic. These tools are unbiased and objective. The problem is, some psychological tests tend to focus on screening people out, not in. They tend to pigeon hole people based on pre-formulated 'correct' responses, without considering the individual."

"Testing is a lot of work—and expense," Dale commented, crossing his arms on his chest. "I tend to use my gut when making my final decision. If I like someone, and we seem to click, then I hire them."

"Intuition can be valuable," agreed Hawk. "But be careful. Too many interviewers are swayed by their emotions, especially by first impressions. Headhunters constantly have to push aside their first impressions of someone in order to objectively interview that person."

Dale objected. "But first impressions *are* important."

"Too important!" exclaimed Hawk. "Emotion clouds judgment. Hiring managers make up their minds about candidates way too quickly, often within seconds of meeting that candidate."

"That's scary," Sue-Lee said.

"It shows the power of first impressions," I said.

"And the danger of the handshake moment," said Hawk. "We're all naturally drawn to people who are attractive, outgoing, confident, and well-spoken. It is said that interviewers often have their minds made up about someone within seconds of greeting them, and then spend the next sixty minutes looking for answers to affirm their predetermined 'yes' or 'no' decision. Always stay open minded and don't make a decision about a candidate right away. Wait until you have gone through an assessment of their skills and past performance before you size them up. That's critical!" Hawk noted that he knew many managers who were pleasantly surprised with the superior performance of some individuals (whom circumstances forced them to hire) even though initially they had serious concerns about them.

"I often pre-screen someone over the phone before I meet them," I said. "That helps me eliminate the bias of first impressions."

"There's only so much you can learn over the phone," said Dale skeptically.

"Maybe," I said. "But it helps. Along with getting to know what they're looking for, I can hear how they communicate. I can get them talking and listen not just to what they say, but how they say it."

"Good," said Hawk. "A phone screening can let you focus on some key technical questions first, without being swayed by someone's appearance. That way you'll only bring in the ones you're absolutely certain are qualified. I stress again: beware of your personal biases."

> In a Harvard study conducted by two experimental psychologists, Nalini Ambady and Robert Rosenthal, people who watched a short video clip of instructors they had never met before gave those instructors almost the same ratings as classroom students who had interacted with the instructors for an entire semester. How long was the "short" video clip? Two seconds. In other words, total strangers were making up their minds about people the same way as those who had known those people for an entire semester did.

Hawk took a sip of coffee before continuing. "Now, there is also another benefit to pre-screening on the telephone. It has to do with time management. Can anyone guess it?"

"If you don't like the person, or it's not a fit with what they're looking for," Sue-Lee said, "then you can get rid of them more easily."

"That's it," confirmed Hawk. "If you keep in mind the value of your five-hundred dollar per hour time, you'll want to do as much prescreening on the phone as you can, so you don't bring in people who end up wasting your time—or theirs, for that matter. If you bring them in, you feel obligated to sit with them for at least thirty minutes, even if you've decided right away that they're not a fit. Thirty minutes! That's a couple hundred bucks of your time."

He rose from the table and looked at us expectantly. "It's time to get going," he said. "Our next challenge will really help nail down what the candidate is looking for. It's the most important part of the whole process. So gather your things. We're going to head back to the cottage and then into the woods."

"Sounds ominous," Dale said.

"Let's just say that after it's done, you might have an axe to grind with me."

* * * * *

Chapter 6—Manager Action Steps

Some suggested actions for proactive managers include:

✓ **Identify their needs**—the crucial component in selling candidates on a job opportunity is understanding their needs. To start, find out what they like and don't like about their current job. Give them a simple sheet that asks them to list job elements they want "more of" and elements they want "less of". Ask them, "If you could magically make your job better, what would you add or take away?" Whenever possible, pre-qualify candidates based on their needs and any possible issues they might have. Keep asking them, "Is there *anything else* wrong with your current job?"

✓ **Ask them directly**—Sometime during the initial screening or first interview, ask candidates to directly list their "job switch criteria" and if you can, ask them also to prioritize the criteria. Use telephone screening to save time and gather information about technical skills without being hampered by a visual first impression. Identify "triggers" that might cause people to consider your job opportunity. Ask them: "Under what circumstances might you consider working for us?"

✓ **ABC (Always Be Closing)**—Good salespeople are continually qualifying customers by asking, "Is there anything else you're looking for?" They will then use "if/then" statements to test the trial offer. Example: "If we can provide _____, then is there any reason why you wouldn't accept this offer?"

✓ **Offer dream jobs**—Be prepared to offer the very top candidates their "dream job" which is a job customized to their particular needs and skills. You can identify their dream job and what you have to do to motivate them by using the "more of/less of" sheet. Educate top candidates about job features and company opportunities that they might not have put on their list because they weren't aware these were possible.

✓ **Don't oversell**—Always make sure the match is a good fit for both parties. There is no point in trying to squeeze someone into a role unsuited for them, because you will quickly earn a reputation. Furthermore, ensure that it is a good fit for you and your organization. Just because someone is the best, it doesn't mean they are the best for your company.

✓ **Involve your employees**—Consider using peer interviews where the candidate's future co-workers do most of the interviewing and assessment. It often allows the candidate to open up but it is also effective because coworkers can be great sales people.

CHAPTER 7

Look out for the Career Chasm

Chapter 7 Learning Goals:

1. Learn which candidates to focus your efforts on. The labor market is full of talent with differing motivations. There are people who are always looking, people that only look when their needs are not being met by their current employer, and people that consistently leverage new opportunities to advance their career as quickly as possible.

2. Learn how to identify a candidate's "career chasm," the gap between where they are now and where they want to be.

> *"Do not hire a man who does your work for money, but him who does it for love of it."*
> **(Henry David Thoreau)**

It was a short trip from town to the cabin and our next excursion. The sun's heat lay thick throughout the forest as Hawk led us along a narrow path pocked with tree roots and jagged rocks. We each carried an axe and a water bottle, as instructed by Hawk, and I could tell that Sue-Lee was somewhat nervous about the challenge. Unable to resist the opportunity to rib me, Dale chattered about the ten points he and Sue-Lee had each collected for finding a teenager.

After ten minutes of brisk walking, Hawk finally stopped before a small, shallow ravine approximately twelve feet wide. We glanced down and saw, only six feet below us, a small brook trickling through a soft, sandy bed of earth.

"The test now," said Hawk, "is a race to see who can bridge this ravine and get across to the other side the fastest."

The three of us glanced at each other, confused.

"Can't I just climb down and up the other side?" asked Dale, as if he were prepared to don his old, muddy football jersey and charge the end zone.

"Nope," said Hawk. "You have to find a log. You can either chop a tree down," he said, pointing to the axes, "or you can use a fallen tree, if you can find one. I'm predicting it won't take you long. This contest will likely be over within ten minutes."

Dale grinned at me, and I could see he felt cocky about this test. His Paul Bunyan size and strength would surely enable him to build an entire log fort atop the ravine before Sue-Lee and I could even figure out which side of the axe head to use.

"Remember," said Hawk, as he waved his watch in the air, "your five-hundred dollar an hour time is ticking. Now, go!"

We were off and running. Axe in hand, I pushed my way through heavy grass and juniper bushes, dodging sixty-foot spruce and poplar trees that would take me an entire weekend to chop down. I headed in a southerly direction, away from Sue-Lee and Dale, hoping to get lucky and spot a decent sized snag—a semi-dead tree hung up in the limbs of other trees. Many branches and slender logs lay on the ground, some the thickness of my forearm, but I knew that they wouldn't hold my weight. I looked up. Many of the smaller, healthy trees were six inches in diameter and I estimated it would take only five minutes to cut one of these down. Clearly the trick with this game was to play the odds: if I could quickly find a small dead fallen tree, then I could have one back and laid across the ravine in no time at all. However, the precious time spent looking for one could instead be used for chopping down a good tree. It was a gamble any way you cut it.

Just then, I heard someone crashing through the forest nearby. It was Sue-Lee, dragging a small log that she must have found on the ground almost immediately. She grinned at me as she struggled past, and I could tell she was enjoying this game. I noticed, however, that her log was small and possibly rotten. She was gambling that this log would hold her ninety-eight pounds. If it did, the game would be over. If it didn't, she would be back in the forest.

I made my decision. I quickly scanned the treetops and then decided I would cut down one of the poplars, which had fewer branches than the spruce trees, making poplars easier to haul. I selected a fifteen-footer nearby, one with fewer trees around it so that it could fall to the ground without getting hung up on another tree. Grabbing the handle of the axe with both hands, I took aim at the base of the tree and swung away.

Now, I'm not much of an outdoorsman, and the last wood chopping that I had done was several summers before when, picnicking with the family, I had used a rusty hatchet to mangle some oak firewood into kindling for a wiener and marshmallow roast. This axe, however, was sharp and heavy, and after chopping a notch on one side of the tree, I made rapid progress on the main cut. Sure enough, within four minutes the tree started to sway, and several swings later it toppled and landed among the moss and soil. I seized the tree by its base and started off. It was hard going. I had to stop several times and whack away several branches that became caught up with other branches or roots along the way. When I finally made it to the clearing and saw Hawk, I estimated that ten minutes had gone by since I had started. Sue-Lee had probably finished by now.

But where was she? I noticed that Hawk was standing at the edge of the shallow ravine, looking down. There was no log across the gorge and none lying nearby, so right away I knew that Sue-Lee's log had not held. I dropped my tree and rushed over to the edge. There she was, sitting on the sand six feet below, brushing dirt and bits of wood off her clothes. The broken log lay in two splintered pieces beside her.

"Are you okay?" I called out.

She nodded and smiled sheepishly. "What can I say? Mine was too small."

"Peter, you better get moving," said Hawk, as he pointed across the clearing to the forest.

I turned to see Dale crashing from the woods in front of us. Like an overloaded lumber truck, he was staggering along with a massively thick log, as round as a bass drum and as long as a sofa. It must have weighed three hundred pounds. Normally it would have taken two men to manage a log that size, but Dale, being Dale, had decided that *this* log had his name on it.

I grabbed my tree and jumped down onto the sand where I reached above my head to maneuver the end of the tree into place on the far side. Within seconds I had it pushed across and secured on the other edge. I could hear Dale's grunting getting closer.

"Oh, no you don't," he hooted playfully. "Here I come to getcha, little man."

As I scrambled back up the bank, I saw Dale muscle the log toward the edge of the ravine. I raced to push my tree a little farther across the gap to make sure it had a solid footing at each end. My log was narrow and I would have to walk carefully across. If it rolled at all, I would lose my footing and tumble off.

With Sue-Lee and Hawk cheering us on, I placed one foot on the tree and tested the stability of it. It seemed fine. I glanced beside me to see Dale standing his log vertically, with one end of the log at the near edge of the ravine, and the other skyward as though raised in a victory salute. All he had to do was flop the top end down and across the ravine. The log's generous circumference and solid weight would allow Dale to practically sprint across … and win.

I stepped out a little farther, one foot in front of the other, until I was a third of the way across, but I knew that I was moving too slowly. All of sudden, I sensed the top end of Dale's log toppling through the air, for a fraction of a second blocking out the sun on my face, before continuing to fall toward the other side. For a moment I thought it was going to fall diagonally onto the end of my tree, catapulting me into the air like one of Dale's schoolyard teeter-totter victims when we were children. Perhaps, I thought, it would be better if it did, so I wouldn't be left standing in the middle of my inadequate log, watching Dale do his victory dance on the other side.

Instead, the end of his log rushed earthward, directly on target with the other edge, down, down—straight past the edge and into the bottom of the ravine where it thudded into the earth and lay still.

It was too short.

In his haste to find a thick, solid log that would bear his weight (and undoubtedly prop up his He-Man reputation), Dale had not paid enough attention to the necessary length needed to span the gap.

That was all I needed. I carefully scurried across my tree with no troubles and, arriving on the other side, I turned to offer my best *in-your-face* grin to Dale, who collapsed to the ground laughing. That was one thing I had to give to him: he was always a good sport. And a good loser, despite not having much practice at it.

"Well done, all of you," clapped Hawk. "And congratulations to Peter who collects ten points to make it a three-way tie in the contest."

Hawk and Dale helped Sue-Lee back up the bank, and she admitted that, apart from her pride, nothing was injured.

"So, what did you learn?" asked Hawk.

Sue-Lee spoke up. "I know what you're going to say about my log. It was too thin. It was like an inferior candidate who can't handle the job."

Hawk nodded. "You're way ahead of me."

"And that there are plenty of them out there lying around," continued Sue-Lee, motioning to the forest. "They're a dime a dozen."

"Yes, and just as there are different kinds of logs, there are different kinds of candidates," said Hawk. "Top headhunters recognize the difference. Let's go sit in the shade and I'll tell you about the three categories of target candidates: the Frequent Lookers, Reasonable Ricks, and Fast Track Freddies."

* * * * *

When we had all settled onto the grass in some shade near the ravine, sipping water from our bottles, Hawk began again. "We all recognize the low-performers that nobody wants to hire. I call them the Frequent Lookers, and they're plentiful. Most are underemployed or unemployed. Some recruiters call them 'active candidates' because they are actively looking for a job by searching through newspaper ads, surfing large job boards, and attending job fairs. And because they're not very good, they frequently return to the job market. Unfortunately, because they *are* frequently looking, you have to be particularly careful with these types."

"Why?" I asked.

"Because, with so much practice, their resumes and interview skills are likely to be superior to most other candidates," Hawk replied. "Sadly, their job search skills are almost always superior to their actual job skills. You might occasionally find an okay performer in the Lookers, but you'll have to sift through a lot of bad resumes and sit through a lot of horrible interviews with people you shouldn't be hiring. Chances are, they won't get the job done properly and will end up letting you down halfway through, just like Sue-Lee's log. There are many of them out there and the easy thing to do is to grab the first one you see and try to make it work. Occasionally it might, but it's a low percentage shot to find a great new hire among these under-employed Frequent Lookers."

"But sometimes we just have to find a warm body," said Sue-Lee plaintively. "Sometimes we have a job to get done, and the longer we leave it open, the less productive our company is. Therefore business expediency prevents us from looking for the perfect candidate every time. Sometimes a low performer will do for the short term. A Frequent Looker might work fine."

"Sure, if it's contract work where you can dismiss them easily," agreed Hawk. "All I'm saying is if the job is really important, don't let the Lookers take up too much of your time and effort. If your recruiting strategy— which we'll talk about later—is designed correctly, you will identify viable candidates before a job opening occurs. And as a result, you won't need to jump at warm bodies."

"So we should avoid Frequent Lookers and instead focus our time on the currently employed top talent?" I said. "That's what everyone is talking about: *Winning the top talent*."

"Well, yes, but there are still important decisions to be made," Hawk said. "There are actually two types of top performers. The first type is extremely aggressive because they are quickly climbing their way to the top. I call them Fast Track Freddies. They are great performers but they can be a bit hard to manage and some turn out not to be the best team players."

Hawk took a drink of water. "I have already said that, generally speaking, the best candidates are not actively looking and won't be quick to take your phone calls, if they take them at all. Fast Track Freddies are going places rapidly, and they know it. They're solid and will always get the job done, but it's a low percentage shot catching them. Why? Because they know they're good and needed within the corporation so they are not checking ads and are not putting feelers out in business circles, so it's difficult to identify them in the first place.

"Oh, you can find them if you put a lot of time into it," continued Hawk, shifting position on the ground. "But even if you end up talking to one of them, chances are they're not going to leave their current company. A Towers-Perrin study released a few years ago stated that 20% of workers were highly engaged in their jobs and not likely to leave anytime soon. I'll wager that most of them are Fast-Track Freddies, employed by companies who are doing anything and everything to keep them happy. And these Fast-Track Freddies often develop an ego that makes them difficult to manage. They end up being like Dale's log."

Dale grunted. "That beast just wouldn't cooperate." Then he grinned. "But it sure felt good going after it."

"That's your pride talking," said Hawk. "All companies want the biggest and the best candidates. They want to land the big fish. And don't get me wrong: when you do have the time and resources to land the big ones, mount them over the mantle for all to see. Announce those new hires with a big ad in the paper. It will let everyone know you're a serious player in the hiring game, and it should attract other top performers. They'll think, 'If Charlie went over to company X, then things must be happening there.'"

"But you're saying don't spend *all* your time going after the big fish. That's your point, right?" Sue-Lee said.

"Exactly," Hawk nodded.

"So if the weak logs and the heavy logs aren't our best

A large veterinary hospital realized that many of the technicians (nurses) who came to work for the practice were only using the job as a stepping stone into other careers. After years of replacing staff, the hospital embraced a new process. All employees in the hospital and subsequent new hires would complete a dream career profile. Twice a year hospital administrators would meet with each employee and review how employees were doing and identify how the hospital could help. The hospital leveraged its connections to secure internships with its accounting firm for technicians pursuing a finance education, coached its employees on applying to medical school, and arranged tutors for students. The result was a large network of alumni who no longer disappeared into the oblivion, but actively referred other potential candidates and customers to the hospital.

bets, you're saying we should concentrate on a third group?" I asked. "Something to do with my log, I'm guessing."

"Right, the third group—the Reasonable Ricks," said Hawk. "In that Towers-Perrin survey, just over 50% of respondents said they were *moderately* engaged in their jobs. So a number of good candidates are, for reasons we'll discuss later, poking around a bit. These are not the Frequent Lookers who are pounding the pavement, chasing job openings, and they're not the Fast-Track Freddies who are extremely hard to find, sell and manage. No, I'm talking about the solid performers with great skills, solid work ethics and terrific attitudes. Recruiting them might be a bit easier because they occasionally drop a word to a few friends or business colleagues that they, while not *desperate* to make a move, are not 100% utilized where they currently work. They are the ones who might occasionally check a professional association's Internet site or return a friendly headhunter's call. Because they're good workers, they still take a bit of work to find, but in the long term, they are the ones that are likely to fill a majority of your jobs."

"How did you come to give them the name Reasonable Ricks?" Sue-Lee asked.

Hawk responded, "Every time you talk with one of these candidates and you ask them if they'd consider making a move to a better position, instead of bluntly saying no, they are more reasonable and instead they generally say ... what?"

"*Maybe,*" guessed Sue-Lee.

"Exactly," replied Hawk. "When you ask them if they'd be interested, they say something like, '*Maybe. I don't know. I'd have to know more about it.*' Or, '*Maybe. I guess if it was my dream job I might look at it.*' These Reasonable Ricks are the ones you want to focus on for the majority of your jobs. They don't come to you like Frequent Lookers but at least when you do get a chance to talk to them, their ego doesn't get in the way of their considering another opportunity with more growth and challenge."

"But a lot of those Fast-Track Freddies might say *Maybe*, too, when you call them," I protested.

"Sometimes, yes," agreed Hawk.

"That is precisely why you have to be careful about whom you target, so that you don't waste your time on people with a low probability of making a move," said Sue-Lee. "That's what we find at our firm."

"Exactly," exclaimed Hawk. "That's why this next point is so crucial. Listen up. You need to learn to pre-qualify like there's no tomorrow, 'cuz if you waste all your precious time on individuals with a low possibility of closure, believe me there will be no tomorrow at your company."

"Pre-qualify," repeated Sue-Lee. "How? At our firm, when we find someone we think is qualified, we tell them about the job. If they're interested, they'll accept."

"You mean you just throw some bait in front of them and hope they bite?"

"In a manner of speaking, yes," she answered.

"If executive recruiters worked that way they'd be starving to death," said Hawk. "Instead, you need to figure out the probability of them moving. That process starts with identifying the width of their career chasm."

We all perked up. "The what?"

"Their career chasm. It's the disconnect between where they are now," he said, pointing to one side of the ravine, "and where they want to get to in their career." With his other hand he pointed at the opposite side of the gulley. "Find out what separates those two spaces and then you'll know if your job opportunity will bridge that gap. That's the key. Every great headhunter knows how to identify the career chasm of a candidate by identifying where they currently are in their career and then discovering what it is on the other side that they're searching for. If your job opportunity doesn't provide those riches on the other side, then don't force a job on them or it will only end up being an unsuccessful placement."

"Riches on the other side?" scoffed Dale. "Half my laborers just want to make enough to buy a case of beer and a pack of smokes at the end of the day."

"Come on," returned Hawk. "You know that's not entirely true. They, like most people, want job satisfaction, too. And job satisfaction comes from achieving things. It comes from having interesting work, from meeting day-to-day challenges, and from being recognized and appreciated for meeting those challenges. You need to talk to those guys and find out what kinds of things they need to accomplish in order to gain that job satisfaction."

"If I start talking to my guys like this, they're going to look at me like I'm a flake," said Dale.

"So don't use these terms that I'm using. Put it in terms they can relate to. And they probably won't be able to articulate exactly what it is they're looking for, so it's your job to keep prodding until you learn what that career chasm is. *That* is the key to getting a candidate to bite. It's the first step in getting them from 'maybe' to 'yes'. If you just start doing a feature dump about the job you're selling, without knowing what will truly motivate and reward the candidate, it could be a waste of your time."

"I don't know," Sue-Lee said doubtfully. "Like I said, if we have a position, we do our best to convince them to take it, and that's it. Either they want the job or they don't."

"I see." Hawk looked up at the deep blue sky. High above us, a tiny glint of silver—a jet no doubt—spun a white gossamer thread between where it came from and where it was headed. "Stephen Covey, author of the classic book *The 7 Habits of Highly Effective People*, identified the single most important principle for effective interpersonal communication: '*Seek first to understand, then to be understood.*' That directly applies when talking to candidates. You have to understand *them* before you can market your job to them. You can't be duplicitous or manipulative with your own goals in mind; you truly have to listen to what *they* need first."

I could see Sue-Lee's resolve softening, but she still looked somewhat defiant. "It still seems like a rather airy-fairy way of hiring candidates," she said.

"I keep telling you, the candidate is the customer now." Hawk then stood up. He looked at us and said, "I want to make a bet with you. I'll wager that we have a couple of Frequent Lookers back at the cabin right now. I'll bet that when we return, those two teenagers you recruited are sitting around doing nothing."

Sue-Lee and Dale looked at one another. "Why do you say that?" Sue-Lee asked. "After all, we're paying them good money. They agreed to do the job."

"Hmph," replied Hawk. "Let's go see."

* * * * *

Chapter 7—Manager Action Steps
Some suggested actions for proactive managers include:

✓ **Focus on high probability candidates**—Like thin logs lying around in the forest, there are plenty of weak candidates about. Stay away from the Frequent Lookers. There is a reason they are beating down your door; they generally turn out to be underperformers. Unless you exceed average selling and retention rates, don't spend too much time recruiting the Fast Track Freddies, the absolute best-of-the-best who are on the way up within their own companies, have no reason to leave, may not be team players, and could be difficult to manage. Instead, build a relationship with these folks and leverage the relationship into a resource. Ask these people for referrals. Primarily target the "Reasonable Ricks" type of candidate. These individuals are not the classic "passive" job seekers. They are great performers who have to be asked directly before they will consider another job. You have a higher probability of 'landing' and retaining these candidates.

✓ **Identify their career chasm**—Prequalify candidates based on the gap between where they are now and where they would like to be in two years in their careers. You can identify where they want to be by using a short questionnaire or an interview (see appendix). If the gap between where they are now and where they want to be won't be significantly filled by this job opportunity, pass on the candidate rather than disappoint them as an employee. Don't just throw an opportunity in front of a candidate before doing market research on the candidate. You do it for customers.... why not for candidates?

✓ **Spend your resources where they count**—Develop a system to track your success rate in attracting and closing candidates. Based on your success rate of landing Fast Track Freddies or Reasonable Ricks, allocate your time and budget resources toward the type of candidate you have the highest probability of landing.

✓ **Measure the quality of hire**—Develop a system of measuring your "quality of hire." Check to see which type of candidate performs best on-the-job. Use performance appraisals or rankings after six months and one year on the job to see which source produces the best results.

CHAPTER 8

From *Maybe* to *Yes*

Chapter 8 Learning Goals:

1. Learn how to differentiate yourself, build your employment brand, and sell your company's unique value.

2. Learn to write goals-based job descriptions that "wow" candidates. The best candidates (Reasonable Ricks and Fast-Track Freddies) need jobs that are gratifying and rewarding. To attract them, managers truly need to look at the job description not as a legal description, but as a *marketing* one.

"It is an old and true maxim that 'a drop of honey catches more flies than a gallon of gall.' So with men. If you would win a man to your cause, first convince him that you are his sincere friend. Therein is a drop of honey that catches his heart, which, say what he will, is the great highroad to his reason, and which, once gained, you will find but little trouble in convincing him of the justice of your cause, if indeed that cause is really a good one."
(Abraham Lincoln)

It was six o'clock, and Dale, Sue-Lee and I sat in the shade of the cabin deck, munching brownies that had been left on the doorstep with a note from Gladys hoping that the treat would "perk up your day."

"Some sweets from your sweetie," Dale had teased, but Hawk had just mumbled something and headed down to the dock to talk with the teens.

Sure enough, as Hawk had predicted, they had finished up their earlier task and were lolling about near the shoreline when we emerged from the forest and walked up on them. They hadn't even seemed embarrassed to be caught doing nothing. Instead, they had glanced at us and then continued staring across the water at town. Whatever their friends were up to, their stares suggested, it had to be more fun than this.

As I relaxed in my chair, I noticed the way Hawk related to them, his hands in his pockets, his eyes cast downward, as if he were taking on *their* body language. Finally, it seemed as though Hawk had gotten through to them, because their faces changed and they suddenly seemed to buy into whatever he was saying. They followed him over to a shed in the bushes, collected rakes, and then began combing the grass for pine cones that had fallen everywhere. They seemed to be working quickly, with a renewed sense of vigor and purpose.

Hawk joined us on the deck and I nudged the pan of brownies toward him. "Have another one," I said.

He stared at it for a moment and then shook his head. "That woman won't be happy until I'm fat and lazy."

Sue-Lee smiled at him. "All the easier for her to catch you then."

Hawk muttered something and went inside. He returned a moment later with an orange and began peeling it. His dog, Scraps, waddled over and flopped down beside me. Unlike most dogs who would sit and attentively stare at my brownie, this dog lay flat on his side, his nose on the floor, his mouth ajar, and one eye staring expectantly up at me as if to say, 'What are you waiting for? Drop it in.'

"What was going on with those kids down there?" Dale asked, motioning toward the water.

"Oh, that," replied Hawk. "It seems that they're bored already."

"How did you know they'd be sitting around doing nothing?" I asked.

"Because you told me that when you found them, they were just standing around doing nothing. They were unemployed, unmotivated, and untalented ... just like most of the Frequent Lookers. Do you recall me saying that the best people are usually gainfully employed and aren't looking for work?"

"That's quite a generalization," Sue-Lee said.

"Yes, it is," conceded Hawk. "But the stats back it up. Once in a while you'll find very talented people who, for whatever reason, are between jobs. However, that group represents a small minority. The majority of talented folks are working. And the majority of the people who are without work for long periods of time, or who have job-hopped from place to place, are Frequent Lookers."

"Maybe so. But what about a sense of obligation? After all, these kids agreed to do the job," I complained. "And we're paying them good money."

A wasp flew by, and Hawk waved it away from his orange. "Money tends to motivate the Lookers more than the other two groups. They'll often accept a job just for the paycheque. Usually that motivation lasts for about the first three minutes, especially with these kids. Then you have to find something else to convince them, something that will 'wow' them. Marketing people are always thinking this way, about branding and positioning the product. In recruiting, your product is your job opportunity. In recruiting terms, marketing means you make your job so appealing to the right people that those people will eagerly move from Maybe to Yes. You need to first isolate the customer's career chasm, and then market around that."

"Career chasm?" laughed Sue-Lee. "These are teens, doing yard work. What kind of career chasm could there possibly be?"

"The principle applies on every level, even with kids doing yard work. You must find out what's going to motivate them and then start positioning your product—your job opportunity. You have to convince them that you have something that is truly in *their* best interests, not just yours. To do that, you need to determine what the *purpose* of the job is. Isolate the top objectives for the job, and make those objectives concrete."

"Yeah, too many job descriptions are just laundry lists of

> A Fortune 500 networking firm in the Silicon Valley hired advertising people to rewrite their job descriptions. Not only were the JDs then more interesting, but they closely followed the needs and the decision criteria of the most desirable applicants.

duties," I said, thinking of all the vague and fluffy ads in the career section of the newspaper each weekend.

"Kind of like the flyer we made up this morning," mused Dale.

"Tell me about that again," Hawk asked. "What did you write on it?

"It said, '*Part time job this weekend only. Great pay,*'" answered Sue-Lee.

"Did you include anything about goals, achievements, and accomplishments?"

Dale's brow furrowed. "No. It's just a job doing some odd chores. It's grunt work."

"Point taken," agreed Hawk. "But *my* point is that this is basic recruiting theory, and it needs to be practiced with all jobs, even junior ones."

"What should we have done with the flyer?" Sue-Lee asked.

"Well, start by thinking excitement," said Hawk. "You certainly want to mention and talk about the things that are likely to excite and motivate potential candidates as well as employees in the job. Think of it as both a sales brochure and a daily motivation guide for employees in the job. Get someone with creativity and personality to write your job descriptions.

"Next," continued Hawk, "expand on the duties by clearly outlining what they'll be striving to achieve, what they'll be doing in the job during the first twelve months. It's important that you include measurable results. If you're detailed like this, then down the road you can also use the job description for performance measurement and merit increases."

"Can you give me an example of a measurable result you'd write in a profile for an accountant?" Sue-Lee asked.

"Let's see," he said after chewing another piece of orange. "Instead of writing something like '*produce month-end financial statements*' as part of the job description, try breaking it down into a smaller goal. You could write '*reduce month-end turnaround time from ten days to five days.*' Or, instead of '*handle all banking*' you could put, '*seek out and negotiate new line-of-credit with the goal of saving the company a minimum of $5K in interest each month.*'"

Sue-Lee returned a thoughtful look. "Yeah, that's not bad."

"I suppose," nodded Dale, half convinced. "But that gets pretty tough to do when it's an unskilled laborer position, let's say a job running a piece of equipment like a loader?"

"Well, on the first day of the job," said Hawk, "what do you tell that loader operator his goal is?"

"We tell them to keep loading the trucks and don't stop until they're full. That's it."

"Do you have some loader operators who are better than others?"

"Of course."

"And what makes them better?"

"They work faster, spill less. They keep their equipment in good shape. Their paperwork is always in order."

"So you *do* have objective performance measures. When that new guy starts his first day on the job, you always tell him what his measurable results should be. You're probably saying something like, '*you need to reduce down-time on equipment by 20%, maintain a load rate of two hundred yards per hour, check your John Deere XJ4 equipment twice daily, and achieve a paperwork error margin of less than one percent.*'"

"Something like that," confirmed Dale.

"So, take those specific objectives," said Hawk, "and add them to your job description. Then, when you're actually recruiting, you can market the opportunity around those objectives and raise the interest of the right person."

"Hmm, I see."

"Writing your job descriptions this way produces several results: One, it will help you weed out the wrong people from applying, both those who cannot accomplish those goals or those who aren't interested because their career chasm won't be bridged by doing those things. You'll be left with people who read it and think, 'Oh, *that* is what this employer needs. I can do that. I *want* to do that.'

"The second result," continued Hawk, "is that you will be providing the applicant time to think about the challenges so that at the interview itself they can start presenting their solutions to the challenges. And *that*, my friends, is how you should be learning about their skills, experience, and other attributes … not from their resumes or from all those other tedious questions that routinely get asked in an interview."

"That's interesting," I mused. "You're saying that we should get them thinking about the challenge in advance and ask them to come to the interview with potential solutions. Won't that scare off some good people?"

Hawk shook his head. "Just lazy people. People who don't like to plan ahead and solve problems. No, good people won't be afraid of you challenging them. Good people have a 'Bring it on!' attitude. They will welcome the chance to prove themselves, especially if it's the kind of challenge they're looking for. It all comes back to the career chasm and how you're going to help them meet their career goals."

"Makes sense," nodded Dale thoughtfully. "With my machine operator, for example, I could bring him in and ask him what kind of experience he's had in the past reducing down time."

"That's right," confirmed Hawk. "You can be much more targeted in your interview questions. And because you've already put that objective in the job description, the applicant will have had to think about his experience ahead of time. He won't be caught off guard."

"Don't we want to see how they react under pressure, with no time to prepare canned answers?" asked Sue-Lee.

"With some positions, yes," agreed Hawk. "But do you really think for a laborer or a lab-tech it's important to have great interviewing and presentation skills? Far too often employers discount or even reject someone who is excellent because that person flubbed the interview."

The three of us sat quietly for a moment while Hawk finished his orange. I thought about my own company and some of the job descriptions we had written over the years, and some of the interviewees we shouldn't have disregarded so quickly.

At that moment, the phone rang inside the cabin. Once again, Hawk dismissed it with a wave, letting the answering machine do its job.

"What I'm teaching you here," said Hawk earnestly, "is how to get candidates from Maybe to Yes by positioning your opportunity correctly. You need to highlight your problems and what your department needs to accomplish. When you present those challenges—be it in the job description or web posting—you must specifically outline what can be achieved, or what type of career chasm can be filled. All you're doing is appealing to the needs of the right individuals at the right time. It's simple marketing."

I let out a small laugh. "I'm not sure what our HR department would have to say about all this. They have a nice little template for job descriptions, and I don't think there's a box on there for career chasms."

"From now on you won't have to worry about that," said Hawk, "because you won't be letting HR write your job profiles any more. Invest the time in writing the profiles yourselves."

"It takes a lot of time to write job descriptions," Sue-Lee said.

"Sure it does. But we're talking about winning a war for talent. Does a general just throw his troops on the battlefield without advance planning? Does a builder let his laborers start constructing a house without a blueprint? Of course not. Winning the battle takes sound knowledge of what the goal is and what is needed to get there. Nobody in the company knows better than you, the department manager, what results need to be accomplished in your area and the exciting and challenging aspects of this job. The overworked folks in HR see a *job* that needs to be filled, while you see the *work* that needs to get done. They see the hole that has to be filled; you see what filling that hole will enable you to get done. You can try to articulate what you need, and sometimes HR will get it right, but often they'll come back with a regular coffee when what you really wanted was a double low-fat decaf mochaccino with sprinkles. Or vice versa."

A gust of wind blew across our faces, and I heard a dog bark several cottages away. Near the shoreline in front of us, one of the teenage boys said something to the other and laughed, while they continued accumulating pine cones.

"So what did you say to those kids just now to get them to keep working?" I asked, looking at the two teens rapidly raking pine cones on the lawn.

Hawk wiped some juice from his hands onto his pants. "I just did a little re-positioning and re-branding, and came up with a USP—a unique selling proposition."

"A what?" said Dale, the one with the least marketing knowledge in our group.

"In the world of marketing, a unique *selling* proposition identifies a void in the marketplace, something that you offer that nobody else offers. In recruiting, that void is the candidate's career chasm. Your USP favorably distinguishes and differentiates you from the competition. With a candidate who is already gainfully employed, that competition is his current employer."

"I've read lots of career ads," I said, "and most USPs are pretty boring. They use generic terms like 'dynamic culture' and 'growth-oriented.'"

Hawk smiled and nodded. "And what's the problem with that?"

"The problem is, everyone is using those words, so they're not unique."

"Absolutely," agreed Hawk. "There is no thought to the U … the 'Unique' in USP. Companies still have an old mentality of 'Well, everyone should want to work here,' so they just throw out a bland 'join our team' message with no promise of something special. Their ads are written with the same rhetoric and jargon that everyone else is using."

"Can you give us an example of a good USP?" I asked.

"Sure. Let's say you're looking for someone who can take over for the department manager who is resigning in a year and a half. Instead of advertising for someone who is 'ambitious' or 'upwardly-mobile' or even 'driven to succeed,' why don't you explicitly state: 'opportunity to advance into the Manager's role within 18 months.' Now, if you're a go-getter itching to climb the ladder, wouldn't that specific wording get your juices flowing a little more?"

"Yeah, but doesn't that potentially create false expectations sometimes?"

"No, that's a misconception," said Hawk. "When it comes to marketing their product or service, companies are super-aggressive about establishing expecta-

> A commercial florist after hearing of an approach one of their clients took decided to try a new method of developing job descriptions, one in which each job requisition was treated as a new product for which a marketing campaign had to be launched. Partnering with their corporate advertising department, the corporate recruiting function crafted compelling campaigns that leveraged the reputation of the clients employees would have an opportunity to work with, and the rare list of materials they would get to use. The campaigns were similar to that you may have seen for the Visa Credit Card. The florist who once was only able to attract local talent now commands the attention of floral designers across the continent.

tions. They'll tell you to the last dime what it will cost and to the last minute when it will be delivered. Marketers will tell you all about the specific benefits, rather than just outlining generic features, because sales training 101 states 'do not *feature dump*.' But when it comes to companies marketing their job opportunities, they do a vague, feature dump, talking about job attributes that could be offered by half the employers in town."

"Companies list desired qualifications the same way, I've noticed," Sue-Lee said. "We're guilty of that, too."

"Many companies do," nodded Hawk. "They'll present them like a list of groceries they're trying to buy, because their viewpoint is job-centric. They'll stick an ad in the career section stating that they're looking for: 'a large ham; medium-sized eggs; one loaf of 100% whole wheat bread.' Then, because they still think they're the buyer, they sit back and wait for the ham, eggs, and bread to show up on their doorstep so they can inspect them and perhaps buy them."

We all nodded, thinking about our own companies. Hawk challenged us once again. "So now that you as the employer have realized you're the seller, not the buyer, what other benefits or USPs could you offer to someone you're trying to woo?"

"Our company has great equipment," answered Dale. He then saw the look on Hawk's face and tried again. "Well, our loaders are Caterpillar 966Bs, almost brand new. People love working with those."

"Is that unique in the market?" Hawk asked. "You're the only one offering that feature?"

"In my industry, locally? Yes."

"Excellent, we have our first example of a hiring USP," said Hawk. "I have one for you. I remember recruiting for a biotechnology company and their USP was the chance for beginning researchers to work under a renowned scientist, one of the top specialists in the world. I was surprised, but I quickly learned that that was a hot button for top candidates."

"I can see that," agreed Sue-Lee.

"What would be a good USP for your accounting firm?" Hawk asked her.

Sue-Lee sat forward. "Our staff often say they feel overworked and burnt out, so we are now offering three weeks' vacation to all junior staff to start, instead of just two. It moves up to four weeks after three years." She seemed pleased to be announcing this. "No other CPA firm in the city is offering this yet, and we're convinced it will help us attract more staff."

"That's great," smiled Hawk. "Now may I ask you a question? If you find an absolute star performer whom you really desperately want to hire, and that junior person says they want not just three but four weeks vacation to start, what would you do?"

She shook her head. "We wouldn't be able to. We have a policy. Others would see that we'd broken it."

Hawk folded his hands behind his head and looked up at the ceiling again. He was silent for at least five seconds, and I was starting to wonder if he had lost interest in the conversation. Suddenly he said, "I want to talk to you about concession planning, but I think I'll wait until later."

"You mean succession planning?" Sue-Lee said.

"No, I mean making concessions, when the fish aren't biting. To move the target candidates from Maybe to Yes, you're going to have to be proactive and consider how flexible you can be with certain things that are important to the candidates."

"Like the compensation package, or flex time?" I said.

"Sure, those are obvious ones," confirmed Hawk, as he stood and stretched. "But we'll talk about that more later on. Right now, all I wanted to do was finish the discussion about branding and positioning your job opportunities. We have covered some good ground. I think you understand what a unique selling proposition is, and how to communicate that USP nicely in a job profile and advertisement."

We heard the teens laughing and roughhousing as they piled more pine cones near the centre of the lawn.

"So are you finally going to tell us what you said to them, Hawk?" Sue-Lee asked, as she pointed at the young helpers. "We're curious how you got them to stay and work."

"I told you, I repositioned the job opportunity. I created a new USP."

"But how?"

"I challenged them. I created a goal for them, something for them to achieve, something that would fill their tiny career chasm at this moment in time."

"More money?" Dale asked.

"Nope. I told them that I had had some of their buddies out here collecting pine cones but that in fifteen minutes nobody had ever collected more than three hundred cones. I told them that if they could collect more than that, then they'd have bragging rights over their buddies. Plus, I said I'd take them into town and buy them jumbo burgers at Alfie's."

I laughed. "Bragging rights and a burger? That's it?"

"You haven't tasted Alfie's burgers."

Dale clapped his hands once. "And what motivates teenage boys more than food?" he said. "On second thought, don't answer that."

We all laughed, and I couldn't help but mentally applaud Hawk for his motivational technique.

Dale stood and looked out at the teens. "But seriously, you're saying a silly little challenge like that is enough to motivate them?"

Hawk winked at Sue-Lee and me and then turned to Dale. "Say, how many points do you have in our contest?"

"Ten," Dale answered quickly, before we saw his face register the irony of the situation. He broke out in laughter. "Okay, you got me."

"Don't underestimate the power of the competitive spirit. Winning can be a huge motivator. Often, especially with the top performers, it's the opportunity to beat the competition and achieve something big that will fill their career chasms."

Sue-Lee nodded and said, "Many CEOs and top executives are marathon runners or triathletes. In business and in their personal lives, they're high achievers and have tremendously competitive spirits."

"I can see that," I said, watching a leaf from above somersault down onto the deck.

"It all comes down to strategy," Hawk responded. "To find the best candidates and then move them from Maybe to Yes, companies are going to have to get more focused and set some goals and targets, just as they would for their marketing plan. That's the next lesson: goal setting. Now, grab your coats while I put some food out for Scraps. We're heading into town for dinner ... and the next challenge."

*   *   *   *   *

Chapter 8—Manager Action Steps

Some suggested actions for proactive managers include:

✓ **Write goals-based job descriptions**: In job profiles, outline the purpose of the job and what specifically needs to be accomplished in the first 6, 12, 24 months. Do this in order to weed out people who can't accomplish the goals or do the job. Instead, find people who will respond with "I can do that. I *want* to do that."

✓ **Create WOW job previews**—Position and market your position opportunity to fit the candidate as you would a product for a customer. Make it so the candidate can immediately envision potential benefits to themselves. To find out what they want, hold focus groups with top performers at industry trade shows and association meetings. Ask top performers what would motivate and excite them about a job. Ask them what words, numbers or features would differentiate a good job from a great job. Then position your job descriptions as ones they'll find gratifying and fulfilling.

✓ **Identify your company's unique features**—Identify your Unique Selling Proposition (USP) by asking your top performers about the exciting and challenging aspects of their jobs. And then work with a copy writer from advertising or marketing to put those aspects into the position description.

✓ **Differentiate yourself**—Compare your job descriptions to those of similar jobs at your direct competitors. Make sure that yours are unique and that they contain differentiators, so that in a focus group, everyone selects your job descriptions as more exciting.

✓ **Build your employment brand**—Work with your PR and product branding department to help determine your brand characteristics and then spread the word within the community about the unique aspects of your job and company.

✓ **Build partnerships**—Smart headhunters don't attempt to do everything alone. Instead, work with a key individual in marketing, advertising, sales, PR and product branding. Study their processes and ask them to teach you the principles and practices of great marketing and selling.

CHAPTER 9

Ready, Aim …

Chapter 9 Learning Goals:

1. Learn to align your recruiting goals with business goals.

2. Learn to develop a written recruiting plan, similar to a marketing plan. Good managers constantly strategize and adapt how they court and retain talent. The goal is to be proactive about leveraging market conditions versus reactive.

3. When top talent is found, it should be courted until such time as it can be leveraged.

"Those who trust to chance must abide by the results of chance."
(Calvin Coolidge)

After grabbing our coats, six of us, including the two teenagers, piled into Hawk's SUV, a large Ford Expedition with leather seats and an unbelievable concert sound system. As we drove toward town, Hawk waved at several neighbors, one who was out fixing a fence, another who was jogging along the road with a terrier beside him. The sun was starting to set, and brush strokes of pink and orange adorned the sky above the lake. Through the open window I smelled freshly mown grass and the scent of lilacs, and I felt the warm air starting to cool down for the night. It was hard to imagine we'd only been here for one day. I knew I'd miss the lake area after I was gone.

"So we've covered a lot of ground," said Hawk as he slowed toward the first traffic light near town. "We talked about finding the unique sell-

99

ing proposition for your job opportunity, and about how to position it with your customer—the candidate. The next thing I want to discuss is where to set your sights for the future; in other words, setting goals and targets."

Dale scoffed. "Every time I make concrete plans, something changes. It never turns out how I expected. It's almost better just to wing it."

"I hear your frustration," said Hawk. "But Richard Worzel, the guy who wrote *Who Owns Tomorrow?*, says the mistake that most managers make is trying to plan for 'the' future, as if there is *one* future ahead and, if you're smart enough, you can know what it is. He says you can't, but that you need to plan anyway, and to adapt when things change. I'm advising you to go ahead and set goals and targets around hiring so you have a starting point from which to work."

"Goals and targets?" Sue-Lee said. "You're making it sound like we can map out our staffing needs. But we can't predict when someone is going to leave and we'll have a hole to fill."

"Not always. But if you look at past turnover and future growth plans of the company, then you can start planning your recruiting strategy," countered Hawk.

I understood Hawk's point right away. "You're saying we can be proactive instead of reactive?"

"Yes. And, as with any aspect of your business, advance plan-

> One major oil company, frustrated with the ups and downs of hiring in the oil industry utilized regression analysis to analyze its past hiring and turnover patterns. The resulting forecasting line helped recruiters to predict future peak and slack periods.

ning allows you to be more precise. It's the difference between using a shotgun and using a rifle," said Hawk. "Your aim is much more precise with a rifle, so you'll end up being more effective and waste less time blasting blindly away at the general marketplace of candidates."

I stole a glance at the teens, and judging by the looks on their faces, they couldn't wait to be dropped off, so they wouldn't have to listen to this boring business talk any longer.

When we reached the center of town, Hawk pulled up beside a small diner with a sign on the window reading Alfie's. "Thanks for helping out today," he said to the two teens, who just nodded and mumbled something. Hawk had paid them their wages, plus given them an additional ten dollars each for a burger and fries at Alfie's. They had collected almost four hundred pine cones and were worn out from their activity. We wistfully said our goodbyes to our only recruits, even though they had turned out to be a couple of underperforming Frequent Lookers. We watched them flee as if they had been freed from a close call with crazed geriatrics. Soon we were out in traffic again driving down the main street toward the beach.

"It's not enough to set vague goals," continued Hawk, as he flipped on his turn signal and turned onto the beachfront avenue. "You have to know which direction you're going. Your goals have to be quantifiable so you can measure them later. It's just like when you run one of your marathons, Sue-Lee. Do you go out and expect to run all twenty-six miles on your first day of training?"

"No, of course not," she answered. "We plan ahead, and set achievable goals and work toward them over time."

Workforce Planning Simplified—A leading expert in workforce planning succinctly described the purpose of planning ahead. You plan ahead because you accomplish more if you are prepared than surprised!

"So the same thing applies here," responded Hawk.

Dale grunted, and I could tell he was about to lose interest. He had never been much of a goal setter or planner back in school, but instead relied on his street smarts, smooth tongue, and physical brawn to barrel his way to wherever he wanted to go.

"There is a man named Edwin Locke," said Hawk, "who is probably the world's foremost authority on goal-setting theory. He says it is crucial to have standards of evaluation. Goal-setting directs effort and focuses attention. It directs the magnitude and form of performance. And the more specific and behavioral a goal is, the greater the likelihood that the goal will be accomplished. But goals do not stand alone. In order to have an effective process, they must be coupled with feedback, or what he calls 'knowledge of results.' Goals alone or feedback alone are not as effective as both operating together. Feedback is also motivational in that it tells you whether you succeed and how to get better. As a result, it leads to future goal-setting, not the other way round."

Dale made a face at me, and I suspected he would rather be with the teens at that moment.

"I can agree on the importance of goal setting," I said to Hawk. "But what is an example of a measurable recruiting goal?"

"Well, let's start in broad terms using turnover as an example. If you historically lose 10% of your staff each year, then you need to plan on a target of hiring 10% new staff this year."

"If we have that kind of problem, shouldn't we be focused on retention first?" Sue-Lee asked.

"Sure, that's very important. But you'll never keep 100% of your staff. There will always be turnover. You'll have underperformers you'll need to let go, or people who are retiring, or people who get promoted up the ladder to more senior positions within the company."

"I guess that makes sense," conceded Sue-Lee.

"You should also tie your recruiting goals to your overall business objectives," said Hawk. "If your company's goal is to grow the business by 12% by year end, then your recruiting goal may be to hire 12% more staff. If you already have 100 people, that's twelve more bodies. It only makes sense that you hire them pretty quickly, say within three months, if you are to reach your growth goal. That timeline might mean hiring four people per month for three months. There, you've got your timeline and your overall goal. Both of these can then be broken down into smaller objectives and turned into mini action plans. Everything is substantive and measurable, from start to finish."

Many firms in service-based industries are already feeling the pinch for labor and shortages at the top have forced professional firms to recruit entry level talent that can be groomed into what is needed. To help counter poaching and demonstrate that recruiting is a shared responsibility one hospitality company recently added recruiting and retention effectiveness as one of the five bonus criteria for all line managers. To establish targets, managers were presented with historical performance numbers across a variety of metrics and asked to set their own goals, which were then reviewed by and accepted or rejected by the CEO.

"How do you create an action plan around *that*? The goal of growing the headcount by 12% is just too broad," Sue-Lee said.

"Nonsense," fired back Hawk. "Start by analyzing the type of talent you need and where you can find it. This is an absolutely vital step. You have to know the kind of people you want, so you can selectively go after them. Remember, it's the difference between a shotgun approach and a rifle approach. If Peter needed a programmer who can write one-hundred lines of Java code error-free in a half hour, then finding that skill set would now be part of his action plan."

"Sure, but apart from the measurable skills, there are always the intangible skills," said Sue-Lee. "Recognizing top performers isn't always easy."

"I know how to recognize them," said Dale with a grin. "I heard a quote somewhere that we don't recognize genius until it goes to work for our competitor."

"I'll grant that," said Hawk, smiling. "Dick Corrick, the NFL scout, used to tell me that defining top talent in the workplace was the same as for pro sports teams. He said NFL teams looked for people of good character who were self-starters, intelligent—people who were team oriented and willing to sacrifice for the good of the whole. People who had that inner drive and the need to achieve. He said that we all instinctively recognize those people around us in the workplace, and so do professional athletes. We just *know* who the superstars are around us. And top performers certainly know other top performers."

"But when we get those names," I said, "I can't just call into my competitor and raid someone."

"Why not?" retorted Hawk. "You're fighting a *war* for talent. Do you think Dick worried about offending other talent scouts when he was helping sign Jamal Anderson, the running back who took the Atlanta Falcons to the Superbowl?"

Dale spoke up. "So how do we go after them?"

"Set sub-goals around this, too," advised Hawk. "One objective might be to make twenty cold calls into competing companies, or to attend two college career fairs each month in order to target students. Or, it might be to get your company placed on 'best place to work' lists in magazines and newspapers, or to establish an internal referral program. All of that goes into your action plan. That's not so hard, is it?"

We had to agree it was not.

"Now here is something else that is important as a goal," said Hawk, as he turned a corner. "One of the most important things you can be doing to help your employees, and hence your company, is to be *continuously* recruiting. That means even when you have no open positions you are constantly looking for talent. In fact the goal is to have every employee a 24/7 talent scout. Continuous recruiting is now essential because the landscape has changed. The talent pool is smaller, plus there is more movement and job changing than ever."

"More movement than back in the late nineties?" I asked. "That was quite a boom time in our sector. Information technology companies were screaming for talented programmers, system analysts, data architects, you name it. If you could spell IT on a resume, then you practically had your pick of jobs out there."

Hawk nodded. "And do you remember what the average length of stay was for people in the IT sector back then?"

"Not long. People moved around every couple of years."

"In fact," said Hawk, "it was fourteen months."

"You're kidding," Sue-Lee said.

Hawk swung the big vehicle off the street into the parking lot of an Irish pub called The Shamrock Shore. "No, I'm not. Today, the job hopping is back, and it will continue to increase in all sectors. Employees will think nothing of test driving a company for six months, and if it's not to their liking—slam!—out the door they go, on to greener pastures."

"So much for loyalty," Sue-Lee muttered.

Hawk shrugged. "You can't deposit loyalty into a bank account."

"Who said *that*?"

"Me, just now," he said, laughing, as he parked the SUV and turned off the ignition. "That Towers-Perrin study I mentioned earlier revealed that 50% of workers were moderately committed to their organization. That sounds good until you consider that the number was 66% in 1991."

> Recognizing the decreased loyalty and increased specialization of talent, one international conglomerate formed an internal re-recruiting team whose goal was to identify valuable talent internally that was likely to be considering leaving and re-recruit them into other areas of the business where their expertise would be of greater value.

"Loyalty really is dwindling then," I said. We all piled out and made for the pub entrance. The breeze, which was starting to cool, felt nice on my skin.

"Yes and no," answered Hawk. "Make no mistake, loyalty is not dead—it's just different. If you listen to Tom Peters, he says that instead of 'vertical' loyalty to a company, young people now have 'horizontal' loyalty to a trade or industry. He envisions a free agent culture, where workers will move from project to project, or Great Gig to Great Gig, as he calls it."

"It's the Hollywood model," Sue-Lee said. "One where workers go from one production to another, plying their trade on that particular movie."

Dale whistled. "That's quite a shift in the traditional workplace."

"Young folks today," continued Hawk, "aren't as motivated by power or money—the two major currencies of the past. Michael Adams, the President of Environics Research, says the younger generation wants 'vitality'—the ability to experience lives of energy and intensity in a more ethical world. They think that *that* is the most desirable end in our society."

Dale looked out at the lake and heaved a sigh. "Quite frankly, I think they're on to something."

"Do you know who the number one private-sector employer in the U.S. is?" Hawk asked. "It's Manpower, a temp agency. That comes from a fellow named Dan Pink who wrote a book called *Free Agent Nation*. Pink says there are between 16 and 25 million freelancers or independent contractors in America. That's a staggering number, one that will likely climb."

"Just great," Sue-Lee said with a tone of dismay. "There's going to be even *more* turnover as more people move into contracting and consulting from permanent jobs."

Hawk held the door for us as we stepped inside. "That's why I keep saying you need to change your mindset about recruiting. As headhunters, you should always be recruiting. And I mean *always*. And it should also be *every* employee's responsibility—through referrals. It should be written into each staff member's job description as a function to be performed on an ongoing basis."

The U2 song, *I Still Haven't Found What I'm Looking For*, was playing as we squeezed through the crowded pub to a table near the back.
Hawk removed a "Reserved" sign and mouthed a silent *thank you* to a
man behind the bar, who gave him a thumbs-up sign. Within seconds, a
young woman was placing drink coasters in front of us. "What'll it be,"
she asked. Dale and I ordered pints of Guinness, while Sue-Lee chose a
gin and tonic. Hawk opted for a single-malt Scotch, with water on the
side. He also ordered four plates of fish and chips, telling us it was mandatory to have that dish when one first came to The Shamrock Shore.

"So, where were we?" asked Hawk.

"You were talking about turnover," said Sue-Lee, "and how one of our
stated goals should be to constantly look for talent in order to combat
the inevitable stream of turnover." A dart thumped into the board on the
wall behind her.

Hawk nodded. "Your target might be to get five referrals each week
and then approach those referrals. Do the math and you would have
headhunted twenty people in one month. Surely five or six people out
of twenty will agree to talk with you. And of that five or six, chances are
you'll hit a bull's eye at least once." Another dart thumped into the wall.

"It will be tough making time for those calls," I said. "I guess I'll just
have to get used to making it a part of my schedule if we want to be successful at finding top people."

"That's the spirit," Hawk said. "The most successful headhunters are
always on the lookout for talent. They're constantly asking others, '*Who
do you know who excels at what they do?*' Instead of being reactive, they're
proactively meeting people all the time, even if there isn't an immediate
opening. They are always keeping their 'inventory' or talent pool full, so
that when a client has a need, they can go to their inventory and produce
a shortlist of suitable candidates quickly."

"But the first thing someone is going to ask when we phone them,"
I said, "is what kind of job opportunity do we have? If we don't have an
immediate opening, why would a candidate agree to meet with us?"

"Because headhunters excel at building relationships with people.
They don't start talking about the job right away. They're candidate-centric instead. They use those candidate questions we touched on earlier:
'*What would you add or take away to make your job better?*' '*If we happened to have a role that is better than your current one, would you be open*

to talking further?' 'Help me understand what kind of role that would be.' I tell you, nobody can resist those types of questions. People are curious. They'll talk with you."

"But I agree with Peter," said Dale. "What if we do get someone interested and then don't actually have a job opening for them? We'll look pretty stupid."

"If that person is a superstar, then make a hole," Hawk said bluntly. "Either by creating a new role or by letting someone else go. It's known as talent swapping."

"You mean fire someone else?" I said. "That's a bit harsh, isn't it?"

Hawk raised his eyebrows. "Are you running a business or a drop-in center?" He then softened his tone. "Jack Welch said GE wasn't doing the bottom performers any favors by letting them plod along thinking they were fitting in."

"What about the other option: creating a new role?" I said. "That sounds like a better idea if we can make it work."

"It sure can be," said Hawk. "Bring a star in, develop her, train her in different areas, and nine times out of ten she will find her proper niche, either because someone else has left or because that new hire has carved a new role for herself."

"You're saying we should just keep focusing on the *person*, not the skill set?" said Dale.

"Right," confirmed Hawk. "In the book *Who Owns Tomorrow?*, Richard Worzel wrote that 'companies need good people more than they need specific skills, especially since good people can learn new skills.' He said we'll witness a *qualitative* shift in how employers and employees interact, which is a key difference from the old model."

"That's expensive," I said, "especially when they don't know how to do the job right off the bat."

"Top talent will start adding value very quickly," countered Hawk. "Remember what I said about the McKinsey survey? Their report concluded that even if you pay an 'A' player 40 percent more to retain him or her, your investment yields a 300 percent one-year return on investment. And another source, Lou Adler, who is one of the top recruiting experts in the U.S, says that the top third of employees outperforms the bottom third by at least 85% in every function. The bottom line is, it just makes an enormous amount of sense to grab hold of a top performer whenever you possibly can."

"That's fine if you have a big company with five thousand employees," Sue-Lee objected, "but we don't have the luxury of paying someone while we let them drift around and find their place."

"Fair enough," agreed Hawk. He sat back and looked at us. "Therefore, another thing you can do when you find someone you really want but don't have an opening for is to court that person until you do have an opening."

"Court them?" Sue-Lee cried.

"That's right. Flirt with them. Look around," Hawk said, motioning at the bar in general. The place was packed with people checking each other out. "Recruiting is almost like courting or dating. Each person has a mental 'list' of what they're looking for—their goals or targets, if you will. If the timing is right, and each party is available and interested in the other, they proceed to start the relationship. But what happens when the timing is wrong? What happens if you do have an opening and there is someone you'd absolutely love to hire, but that person is not interested at the moment?"

Dale shrugged. "There's not much you can do. If you've tried everything you can, and you still can't get them to bite, why waste time trying to catch them?"

"I think I know where you're headed with this one," Sue-Lee said. "You're saying, maybe we'll have an opening in the future, and it's good to stay in touch with, or 'flirt' with, that person for when that day comes."

"Right," said Hawk. "If you're really impressed with someone and would love to hire that person someday, keep that person in mind for the future. Even if they're in a current relationship—in other words, they're employed elsewhere—don't hesitate to stay in contact with that person. I call it 'personal courting.' Remember the candidates are now the customers, so it doesn't hurt to meet them for coffee, take them for lunch once in a while, send them flowers or chocolates on special occasions … just like you

A major Midwestern bank builds a relationship with each of its targeted prospects by sending them a card and a cookie both on their birthday and on New Year's Day—the two precise days that most individuals rethink their life and their future.

would with a traditional client. Let her know you're still interested in her, and that if her situation ever changes then she should call you. Believe me, it can be worth it."

This last comment was spoken with a touch of melancholy, and I wondered about Hawk's late wife, and if he had had children of his own.

"I never thought of that," said Sue-Lee. "I suppose it's flattering for the candidates."

"Of course," said Hawk. "Flattery will get you everywhere. People want to feel wanted. That's part of the whole dating thing."

"Can I play the field?" chuckled Dale mischievously. "You know, romancing more than one candidate at a time. Or is that cheating?"

Hawk laughed. "You should be courting all kinds of people at once. You're not going to hire all of them, so it's imperative that you keep your pool of talent as large as possible at all times. Remember, always be recruiting. Don't wait until you have that round hole before you go looking for the round peg. Go ahead and start talking to the super pegs. And then when you learn what they're looking for, make a hole for them to fit in."

Our food came and we ate hungrily, hardly speaking until the last delicious bite of breaded halibut was done.

"You said we had another challenge in the contest," Dale reminded Hawk as he finished his last homemade fry.

I groaned. "After all that food, I'm not sure I'm up to kicking Dale's butt. But I suppose if it's gotta be done...."

"Tell me we're not going fishing again," Sue-Lee said, looking out the window at the blackness.

Hawk wiped a spot of grease from his mouth and pushed his plate away. "No, we're all done fishing. This next contest is the second last one."

Dale took a playful swipe at me. "Hah, you might as well sit this one out and watch the master at work."

"I doubt it's a sausage-eating contest," I fired back.

"What do you have in mind, Hawk?" inquired Sue-Lee.

He looked at his watch. "For the next hour, from eight to nine, you'll be doing a scavenger hunt of sorts. Only you have to find people in this bar, right here. I'll tell you what kind of people you're supposed to 'collect' and your job is to find them and introduce them to me."

"What types of people?" Sue-Lee said.

"There are three categories. The first is someone who just started a new job. The second is someone who was just promoted. The third is someone who just received a bonus or award due to achievement on the job."

We all groaned, anticipating how uncomfortable we were going to be with this challenge. However, I saw the method to Hawk's madness. It was to get us used to approaching people—or 'cold calling' them—and to give us practice asking some of the questions he was teaching us in order to identify top performers.

"How many points for each person we find?" I asked.

"Each person will earn you five points in the contest total," Hawk answered. "But one other thing: you'll get five bonus points whenever you find out anyone's career chasm."

I took two quick gulps of my beer, as if to fortify myself. Before I could stand, Sue-Lee beat me to it. She smiled at us and, with a gleam in her eye, said, "Well, if I'm going to win this thing, I better get started."

* * * * *

Chapter 9—Manager Action Steps

Some suggested actions for proactive managers include:

✓ **Align recruiting with business goals**—Determine the overall goals of your business and tie hiring in. (Example: if your business goal is to grow by 15%, you may need 15% more staff). Also look at how your boss's performance is measured and rewarded. Use these factors and goals as a baseline to see if you need to revise your recruiting and retention approach to better meet the needs of the business. Realize that, as a manager, you are responsible for the company's success ... and success depends on having the right people at the right time.

✓ **Develop a written strategy**—If you don't already have one, begin developing an overall recruiting strategy. Tailor its design after that of your product marketing plan. Include as an essential element building a strong employee and non-employee referral network, since referrals from top performers are invariably the best way to identify and recruit top talent. After you develop your recruiting goals, make sure there is a measure and a process to monitor each one. Have a feedback loop in your recruiting plan to provide for areas of improvement.

✓ **Establish concrete objectives**—Create an action plan with measurable objectives and timelines. If your goal is to add 15% more staff, your objective might be to make 5 recruiting calls per week.

✓ **Demand accountability**—Work with HR to ensure that every manager is held accountable for great recruiting. Make sure they are measured and rewarded based on how well they recruit, develop and retain top performers. Be accountable for hiring top performers. Add it to your, and every hiring manager's, performance appraisal.

✓ **Anticipate**—Assume that recruiting will become more difficult and that turnover rates will increase dramatically as the economy heats up. Forecast the hiring you'll need to do as a result of turnover and then add to that the hiring needs as a result of corporate growth.

✓ **Be continuously recruiting**—Develop prospects and build a talent pool long before you need to hire anyone. Use personal courting to build a relationship over time with good people. Periodically send them a newsletter, e-mail, card, or gift to keep their interest up. Proactively meet people all the time even if there isn't an immediate opening. And when you find superstars when you don't have an open requisition, have the courage to create a new position for them (or let a poor performer go).

✓ **Don't forget retention**—Develop a retention program that focuses on increasing the amount of challenge, growth and learning that key employees receive. It's also important to realize that "bad managers" are the root cause of most turnover.

CHAPTER 10

Weigh and Measure Your Catch

> *Chapter 10 Learning Goals:*
>
> 1. Learn the importance of measuring recruitment efforts and results. If you are going to take recruiting and retaining top talent seriously, you must be prepared to keep score (i.e. measure your performance).
> 2. Learn which metrics to measure, and how to measure them.

"Measure not the work until the day's out and the labor done."
(Elizabeth Barrett Browning)

The recruiting hour in the pub passed quickly, and before I knew it Hawk was gently tugging at my sleeve, telling me that time was up. I quickly introduced Hawk to a sunburned young man in a Hawaiian shirt with whom I was talking, then gave the man my business card, confirmed a few details, shook his hand, and excused myself.

I made my way back through the sweaty crowd to our table. Sue-Lee and Dale were grinning at each other, and I could tell that they had been comparing notes and tallying points. During the hour I had seen them talking to quite a few people, using a similar line to mine, which was, "Excuse me. I'm conducting a survey, and I just want to ask a couple of questions." I knew that they had met with some success.

"How did you guys do?" I asked.

"Hand me the bassinet, 'cuz this baby's all wrapped up," taunted Dale. He told me that he had talked with more than twenty-five people and had found at least seven who fit into one of the categories. "Sue-Lee only found four," he said smugly. "I get thirty-five points. She gets twenty. That means I'm in the lead with forty-five points total."

Hawk confirmed this, stating that he had met each person. He then added, "But Dale, you forgot about the bonus points I give out."

Instantly the grin disappeared from Dale's face. "What?"

"Remember, the five additional points I award when you take the time to find out someone's career chasm," Hawk said. "Sue-Lee was able to learn what that career gap is for all four of her people. She collects forty points total and, if my math is correct, she moves ahead in the overall contest at fifty points total."

"Ah, crap," said Dale, suddenly deflated. He looked like a little kid whose bright, shiny balloon had just popped.

"How did you do?" Sue-Lee asked me with a grin.

I recounted how I had talked to fewer people than they had—probably only about seventeen—and that I had rounded up and presented to Hawk four people, two of whom had recently been promoted, one who had just started a new job, and one who had just won an employee recognition award. I also explained that I had uncovered the career chasm for three of them. "I believe that's worth thirty-five points," I declared.

"That still puts you in a tie for second with me ... five points behind Sue-Lee in the overall standings," chortled Dale. "She has fifty, and we have forty-five."

"Actually, there is one little achievement that Peter managed that you two did not," said Hawk. "He actually has a real, live candidate whom he will be interviewing at his office next week when they both return to the city." Hawk pointed to Mr. Hawaiian Shirt who was now holding a frosty mug of beer against his sunburned cheek. "And for that, I'm awarding him five extra bonus points. Peter and Sue-Lee are tied with fifty points total, with one challenge left to go."

A major international shipping company's HR measurement slogan reads: "In God we trust; everything else we measure!"

I have to admit that a wave of self-satisfaction swept over me, and I couldn't stop smirking at my two comrades across the table. Sue-Lee laughed and congratulated me, while Dale good-naturedly howled "Fix ... fix!"

We ordered another round of drinks and when they arrived we toasted our overall efforts. The room, while hot and muggy, seemed suddenly more festive, like a party atmosphere.

Hawk looked at us. "What we have just done is evaluate your success in this particular challenge. Measuring and scoring your performance is a critical part of your recruiting efforts."

"Just like any part of our business," Sue-Lee said. "We need to monitor results and track effectiveness."

"You got it," Hawk replied. "Planning doesn't amount to a hill of beans unless you actually *take* action. But action without evaluation is for fools who enjoy repeating mistakes. Like good coaches or good military leaders, good managers are continually assessing what works, what doesn't, and then making adjustments to improve things."

"So, using your examples," said Dale, "let's say fishing for instance—we should evaluate which fishing holes were best and which lures worked."

"And then we need to weigh and measure our catch," I said. "That's part of evaluating results."

"Absolutely," confirmed Hawk.

Sue-Lee nodded enthusiastically. "With hiring, we should analyze the return on investment. In our business, we simply look at chargeable hours and recovery rates on each staff member."

"Good example," said Hawk. "It is tough, but still important to measure the return on investment of human capital. Many articles and papers have been written about ROI. I'm no expert, but I can tell you once again that everyone recognizes top talent, just like everyone knows who the superstars are on a pro sports team. The difficulty is that not everyone can make the business case and show the dollar impact of great hiring and retention."

"So what are some of the other ways to measure recruiting success?" I asked.

"When I was recruiting, the first thing I did after a successful placement was assess how long it took to bring someone on board, and what resources were expended," said Hawk. "Headhunters call it measuring 'time to hire' and 'cost of hire.' The more of your five hundred dollar per hour time you're burning up, the costlier it is. You want to do it right, but do it quickly."

I scratched my head, not liking where this was going. "But so much about recruiting is out of our control," I said. "What if we make our twenty headhunting calls each month and still don't get any nibbles? What if someone is on vacation, and we can't coordinate interviews right away? What if the candidate turns down the offer?"

Hawk nodded patiently. "Those are all very valid points. But in the new war for talent, you're going to 'own' the hiring process, remember? So you'll need to manage that entire process very carefully, just as you'd manage, say, delivery of goods to your customer. Excuses don't hold much water in the world of supply chain management, do they? Either the shipment is there on time or it's not. People get measured on that, and it has become a standard part of goal setting for companies."

I had to admit he had a point. But the thought of having yet another measurable target was daunting.

"Now, here's something else you may not like," said Hawk. "Measuring the time to hire and the cost of hire is the easy part—but those two measures are becoming increasingly insignificant. Instead, you need to focus on measuring post-placement success. In other words, what happens after the hire? Most people fail to measure the quality and productivity of the people they hire. I prefer to use the term 'performance of new hires' but, in either case, it is a feedback loop that tells you if the people you *thought* were top performers as recruits actually *became* top performers. Data on the 'quality of hire' can also be utilized to narrow down and eliminate ineffective sources and recruiting tools."

Sue Lee interjected "Measuring the *quality* of the hire? Come on, that's tough to do. Can't we just track how many new hires stay or get fired?"

"Sure, but the less you measure the less you learn. And the less you learn, the less you improve," Hawk answered. "Measuring their *productivity* is the real key to determining return on investment. Great hires are productive and they increase the overall productivity of the team."

"Yeah," piped up Dale. "I've got some workers who are excellent and others who can barely operate a knife and fork never mind a three-ton piece of equipment."

"There are different ways to measure post-hire recruiting success." Hawk held up his fingers and began counting off. "The first one is the length of time it takes the new hire to begin contributing effectively, which is called 'time to productivity.' The second one is how many people make it past the probationary or initial assessment period. I'm talking about both employer-initiated resignations and employee-initiated resignations. Either way, if it happens during the probationary period, headhunters call it a 'fall-off.'"

"You're saying we should start keeping track of this and deduct points every time someone departs?" Sue-Lee asked.

"Yes," Hawk confirmed. "Now, the third one is quite important. It's the percentage of your hires who become star employees. You can rate your staff and score your success according to how many great performers you have hired.

"The fourth and final one," he went on, "has more to do with long term retention, but it's important to set goals and targets around this, too. You need to measure the number of star performers you lose each year, or 'voluntary departures.'"

"I hear what you're saying," I said, somewhat unconvinced. "But all this setting targets and measuring goals … it would take up a lot of our time and energy."

"So would failure," Hawk said, letting his words hang in the air.

Finally, Sue-Lee leaned forward to say something to Hawk. "You've talked about evaluating the post-placement success of recruiting efforts. A lot of that comes down to whether or not we decide to keep the person, based on their productivity, contribution, and attitude. But when we hire a great person who ends up leaving *us*, that's not really *our* fault. So why should we be measured on that?"

"It's the same as point number two," Hawk said, as he motioned to the server for our check. "It doesn't matter whether you've fired them or they have quit; it was not a successful placement if the position becomes vacant within the first three to six months. And if the employee chooses to leave, you should see that as a failure on your part to assess or place them properly."

"How so?" I asked.

> The individual recruiters at one financial institution are held accountable for new employee turnover within the first six months after a hire. If a new hire leaves, it counts against the recruiter's bonus (yes, some in-house recruiters get a performance bonus, like headhunters). The net effect is that corporate recruiters mentor and stay in touch with new hires, which has the net impact of reducing their failure rate.

"Because it usually happens when the employer has oversold the opportunity, or couldn't deliver what they said they would. The employer overbought."

"They did what?" Dale asked.

"It's an important lesson. When it comes to finding people who fit, don't overreach. For example, don't place an employee with a manager who is not compatible. What that means is, don't hook a fish you can't hang on to."

"You mean we need the right test line or the fish will snap it," I said.

"That's part of it," said Hawk. "What I mean is, I was out on the lake in a canoe with a friend once, and he hooked on to a pike that we could tell right away was huge. My buddy was whooping and hollering, having the time of his life as he fought to bring the thing in. Ten minutes later, when he finally tired the pike out and had it close to the canoe, we could see that it was a beauty. It had to be sixteen pounds—one of the biggest I had ever seen in this lake. I was scrambling to get the net underneath it in the water, and John angled it into the net where it splashed. I was about to pull the net up. The only problem was, we had a weight issue."

I frowned. "The fish's weight?"

"No. John's weight," laughed Hawk. "He was leaning too far over the boat to stare at his prize catch and the canoe started to tip. We were about to go over. In a split second decision, I had to let go of the net and he had to let go of the fishing rod in order to grab hold of the edges of the canoe. Within seconds we were stable again, but the rod was gone. The pike was big enough and strong enough to pull it under the water and take off. He probably died within a week with that hook still stuck in his mouth and a fishing rod trailing him around."

"That's sad," said Sue-Lee.

Dale shook his head. "Ever seen a pike? They're real ugly."

Our server appeared at the table, collected our empty glasses, and set a check down. Before I could reach for it, Dale grabbed it and handed it back with his credit card. We thanked him.

"My point is this," continued Hawk. "The fight to land a new star performer may be thrilling, and you can't wait to tell everyone about your new hire. But first think about whether or not you're equipped to handle it."

I said, "Sure. In business, managers often think that all they need to get to that next stage is one key hire. But if you're not ready for a top performer, it will be disaster."

"Right. Over and over I have seen companies hire star performers, only to have the stars leave within six months. Why? Because the organization didn't have what it took to hold onto them. The hiring managers oversold them on the opportunity and the new hires very quickly found out that the company couldn't deliver on its promises. It didn't have the right product, the right production, the right distribution channels, the right sales force, the right marketing strategy … the list goes on. There could be many reasons why they weren't prepared to handle the top performers."

"The boat has to be stable," said Sue-Lee.

Hawk gave her a nod of appreciation. "That's right."

"But don't companies usually hire someone to help fix a problem? Heck, that's why we hire half our sales people—to do a *better* job than the last person."

"Listen, all I'm saying is that you need to carefully analyze two things: are they a good fit for you, and are you a good fit for them? Most companies focus on the first part. They spend all their time interviewing, testing, doing reference checks, all in an effort to determine if the person is someone who best meets *their* corporate needs. But companies rarely determine if their organization is truly a good fit *for the new hire*."

"We try to," I said. "We tell them about the company, encourage them to talk to people, to do their own homework."

"But what does that mean?" barked Hawk. "It puts the onus on the candidate to figure things out. Then, if it doesn't work out, you can use the cop out, 'Well, I guess they weren't right for our company.' Remember, the candidate is the customer now. You'd never treat a new client that way. You'd always do everything you possibly could to make them satisfied."

"So the onus is on us to ensure a good fit?" I said.

"It's a shared responsibility, of course," said Hawk. "But as the insider, you know what the company culture is like. Candidates don't. You don't want them getting into the job and finding that the culture is not a natural fit. They'll behave unnaturally, trying to adapt themselves, and—voila—you've got an unhappy new hire coping with that nasty adaptive stress syndrome you don't want."

"Doesn't the individual make that choice early in the process?" I asked. "After all, they wouldn't apply in the first place, or go to second or third interviews if they thought it wasn't a good fit."

"Yes, but it's important to remember that companies always put their very best foot forward during the hiring process, so whether intentionally or not, there might be some misleading going on."

"And sometimes candidates see what they want to see," added Sue-Lee.

"Agreed," said Hawk. "It happens all the time. Companies portray themselves in a radiant light and put a positive spin on the job and the vision ahead. But if they *really* know their company—and I mean inside-out and backwards—only then will they know if they are overreaching and if they are hiring someone who won't stick around very long."

The three of us nodded, slowly taking this all in. Suddenly I noticed Hawk's neighbor Gladys enter the pub with several other ladies. She waved at us and smiled, then proceeded towards the bar.

"So," continued Hawk, "now take what I have just said and imagine a scene where a top company is trying to recruit a top performer. *Who* should be involved with the recruiting for the company?"

Sue-Lee snapped her fingers. "A top performer."

"Why?"

"The strong gravitate to the strong."

Hawk nodded. "That's right. There's a quote by Sir Arthur Conan Doyle. 'Mediocrity knows nothing higher than itself, but talent instantly recognizes genius.' That occurs on both sides of the fence. If your star candidate is sitting across the interview table from a mediocre performer, chances are that person will walk."

"But, on the other hand, a star employee will set the bar high, appealing to the star candidate," I said.

"That's right," said Hawk, warily keeping one eye on the bar.

"But my best people are my best billers," said Sue-Lee. "If I keep taking them off files in order to do recruiting, our revenue will drop."

"Temporarily," rejoined Hawk. "Remember, one of my key points in this whole weekend is that if employees are your number one asset, then recruiting must be a priority. And that means putting your best people on it. This is a major shift in corporate thinking, but it has to happen if companies want to be successful."

We looked up to see Gladys suddenly standing at our table. She put her hand on Hawk's shoulder. "Are you talking business again?" she tut-tutted, with her thousand-watt smile "My goodness, Hawk, why don't you give these poor people a break?"

"Would you like to sit down?" Sue-Lee asked. "Hawk can slide over."

"No, thank you anyway," she replied. "I'm with my friends. We stopped by for a quick spritzer before we head over to the community league. They're replaying *Bridges of Madison County*. I just love that old movie, don't you?"

"One of my favorites," agreed Sue-Lee. "I especially liked that Clint Eastwood character. Rugged exterior, but a softie inside."

I smiled at Hawk, but he refused to make eye contact with anyone. When Gladys was gone, Dale poked him in the ribs. "Hey, Clint. Do you want to cut this short and head over to the community league?"

"Don't be ridiculous," Hawk replied. "I told you, we're just friends." He motioned at our server again, and the young woman finally returned with Dale's credit card and the processed receipt.

"Gladys is sweet," said Sue-Lee.

"And attractive," I added.

"She's all over you, buddy," Dale cackled.

Hawk waved away our comments. "I wouldn't know what to do with a woman like that," he muttered. "Besides, she has several suitors in town."

"Maybe she hasn't found the right fit yet," offered Sue-Lee, winking at Dale and me. "Maybe she's a star candidate looking for the perfect offer."

"Yeah, well ... we'll see," said Hawk absently. I noticed that in his hand he had balled up a napkin, which he now tried to hide in the middle of the table between the salt and pepper shakers. "Let's finish off this discussion," he said, changing the subject. "Evaluating the hiring process is important. And—"

"And 'quality of hire' is the most important thing to focus on when tracking success of the placement," said Dale. He signed off on the credit card receipt, and I noticed that he left a generous tip for our server.

"Right," said Hawk. "But so far I have just talked about evaluating your success, about weighing and measuring your catch—the new hire—and tracking the success of your overall recruiting goals and targets. Part of the evaluation process in any company is adapting and making changes when something isn't working."

"Let me guess," said Dale. "That's what we're covering next?"

"You got it. And with it comes our final challenge. It's a close contest, and it's still anyone's game. Let's go."

* * * * *

Chapter 10—Manager Action Steps

Some suggested actions for proactive managers include:

✓ **Make metrics a requirement**—Agree upfront that you cannot improve anything unless you measure it. Metrics in recruiting becomes the key feedback tool for continuous improvement. Dollars and numbers are the language of business and recruiters are not exempt from using the language. For every major goal you set, develop a measure or metric. Create and maintain a companywide recruiting scorecard because "whatever you measure, improves."

✓ **Build a business case**—It's important to build a business case for great recruiting by turning all of your measures into dollar impacts. Calculate the ROI and demonstrate that hiring top performers in has a significant business impact over hiring an average person in the same job. Demonstrate that great hires are more productive than average hires and show the dollar difference between them. The language of business is dollars and numbers, so use these as your measuring units. Instead of measuring cost per hire measure the cost of a bad hire.

✓ **Measure quality of hire**—The most important metric is the quality of hire, which means the relative success rate of new hires on the job. If you only measure one, measure the most important one: *performance of hire.*

✓ **Measure productivity**—After the quality of hire, the most important indicator of great recruiting and retention is to *improve workforce productivity.* It's essential that managers monitor that in order to determine the real ROI of recruiting.

✓ **Track customer service**—Periodically survey a sample of applicants and new hires to see if they are satisfied with the recruiting process. Then examine your present recruiting process in order to identify areas where applicants can be given more say.

✓ **Other things to measure**—Don't forget to measure important things like diversity, new higher retention rates and time to productivity. Also measure and track the most important things to your business. For example, measure sources that yielded top performers, satisfaction both of the hiring team and the candidate, retention rates and mission critical positions filled.

✓ **Rewards are also important**—In addition to measuring success, it is important that you also reward your recruiters and managers for meeting their goals. Reward everyone who helps to recruit, develop and retain top talent! People do what is measured and they do it faster if it is also rewarded. If you care about something (performance of the hire) you need to measure and reward it, just as external headhunters work harder because of their reward structure.

CHAPTER 11

Concession Planning

Chapter 11 Learning Goals:

1. Learn about 'concession planning' (being flexible, adapting, and considering alternatives). If you succeed in getting top talent to the door, but can't close the offer, you need to concede on either the offer itself, the design of the job, or the talent profile you are after.

"The reasonable man adapts himself to the world;
the unreasonable one persists in trying to adapt the world to
himself."
(George Bernard Shaw)

We exited the pub and crossed the street toward the beach. The last building before the beach was a trendy restaurant named Billy Brine's, an ironic name given that the closest saltwater brine was hundreds of miles away. Beyond the restaurant stretched a long promenade overlooking the sandy beach below. It was a concrete sidewalk, well-lit with streetlights and decorated with hanging pots of flowers that the town had placed along the way. After the confines of the pub, the air felt clean and refreshing, although I could faintly smell smoke from several bonfires blazing on the beach. I could hear singing and someone badly strumming a guitar for a small group of people around one fire.

"Back there in the pub," said Hawk, gathering steam again as we walked, "I talked about evaluating your success, about weighing and measuring your catch, and tracking the success of your overall recruiting goals and targets. I said you should be scoring your own success in reaching your targets and timelines, just like you would in other areas of your business. If you don't do this, you're just throwing stuff at the wall and hoping something sticks."

"And if our score is low?" Sue-Lee asked.

"You better hope that you're the boss," laughed Hawk. "But seriously," he continued, "I want to bring up something else now. It's the second part of the evaluation process."

"You mean modifying goals and targets when they're not working?" I said.

"Exactly." Hawk turned to Dale and asked him, "What would you do with other parts of your business if your evaluation revealed that things were not going well?"

"Make changes and adapt," said Dale.

I thought of all the ups and downs Dale's company had endured over the years, and I knew he was probably the most resilient and adaptable of the three of us.

"And what would you do if a customer survey revealed that your customers wanted red and you were delivering blue?"

"Start delivering red," said Dale.

"That's what most people say," Hawk answered. "But the right answer is, 'Start delivering red *if* it makes sense for your company. In many instances it will make sense. And this is where *concession planning* comes into effect."

As he talked, he led us toward a small tourist attraction at the end of the promenade: a paddock with three ponies looking solemn and

A global PR and Marketing firm recognized that despite all the due diligence it conducted during the candidate assessment process, from time to time it was likely that some mitigating factor would result in a mismatch between the new hire and the employer. Now, to help determine how better to sell the opportunity from the candidate's perspective, all new hires are periodically surveyed to gauge their actual experience versus what they anticipated. Gaps are investigated to determine if some aspect of the company needs to change, or if the gap is a one-time incident caused by the peculiarity of a specific candidate. When gaps are too big to overcome, and one or both parties decide to sever the relationship, they reward the new hire for their honest feedback by providing severance packages for both voluntary and involuntary separations.

bored. A single light illuminated the enclosure, and I could smell the pungent aroma of horse manure and hay.

"If your assessment reveals that you are headhunting a sufficient number of top performers, and you are getting a sufficient number to the negotiating table but they're still not accepting your offer of employment," said Hawk, "then you need to start thinking about that C word again— Change. You need to start adapting, and consider how flexible you can be with certain things that are important to the candidates. Remember, recruiting is just like sales. And in sales, closing is an art form, something that requires continuous adjustment and change."

"Should we change the obvious ones we touched on, like compensation packages and flex time?" Dale said.

"Or telecommuting?" Sue-Lee offered.

"Yes, those are great examples. Quality of life and work-life balance seem to be huge priorities for younger people these days. So, if a young mother wanted to work from seven until three so she could be there when her kids got home from school, why wouldn't you concede that, if you *really* wanted that person on your team?"

"That can be disruptive. Others start grumbling about preferential treatment."

"You may be surprised. People are generally understanding and supportive if there are legitimate reasons for things. Furthermore, if there is still grumbling, then find out who is grumbling. If it's a star performer, give that person what he wants, too. If it's someone you don't care to keep, either let him go or lay down the law. Performance matters and top performers get treated differently."

Dale slapped his fist into his other hand. "I had a young mother working as an admin assistant who quit on me two months ago. She said she found a job elsewhere for only five mornings per week. Nobody has ever worked those hours in my company, so I never even considered trying to match that schedule. I just wished her well and she was on her way. I had my blinders on."

Hawk nodded. "There was a CBC survey a few years back. 35% of the respondents said they would take a job with fewer hours for less money. Can you believe it? 35%! To me, that is an alarming statistic."

"So more than one third of my workforce would switch jobs in order to work fewer hours?" said Sue-Lee. "That's incredible."

Hawk waved hello as we approached a young man leaning on a fence of the horse paddock. "The good news is," Hawk said to us, "it is not too late to talk to the rest of your staff and find out if they're content with their hours." He turned to me and said, "What else? Are there any other concessions or unique selling propositions an employer can offer when marketing a job opportunity to top talent?"

"A few of my company's software competitors have in-house gyms and day care facilities," I said. "Most of them have pool tables and cappuccino machines and free snacks. They make their staff comfortable so they like being there."

"Sure," said Hawk. "One software company I know has all of that, plus they even have sleep rooms where employees can take naps if they need to. That entire package of on-site amenities is part of their unique selling proposition when attracting employees."

"You're saying I should serve coffee and other free stuff to my staff while they sit in front of a big screen TV all afternoon?" Dale said. "What am I, Santa Claus, now?"

"It's proven that employees rarely abuse the privilege," Hawk said.

"Yes, but even so, the costs of doing these things must be prohibitive," Sue-Lee said.

"Yes," I agreed. "A fitness facility or day care can be very pricey."

Hawk nodded. "It doesn't make sense for every company to do that. But for some, the capital outlay will pale in comparison to the cost of losing good staff. Remember the McKinsey stat that said that an A player is 50 to 100 percent more productive than an average player."

"So, we need to be more flexible and give the people what they want?" I said. "Power to the people."

"In a manner of speaking, yes. That is the start of concession planning," confirmed Hawk. "Now wait here for a moment. I'll be right back." He walked over to the paddock gate and spoke quietly for a moment with the attendant. It was clear that Hawk had pre-arranged something, because the young man just nodded and pointed a few times, as if confirming that everything was in place and ready to go.

Hawk returned to us and said, "Okay, welcome to the final challenge. It is directly related to concession planning, to being flexible, adapting, making changes, giving up certain things in order to get back what you want." He motioned to the three small horses within the paddock and then pointed to a small ditch that had been dug out on the beach twenty yards away. Something shiny sat on the sand on the other side of the ditch. "Your task," said Hawk, "is to lead the pony out of the paddock, across the beach, and over that small gulley where there is a pail of water. You've heard the old saying, 'You can lead a horse to water, but you can't make him drink.' Well, to win ten points in this challenge, you must both lead your pony to water *and* get him to drink."

"No problem," brayed Dale, sizing up his little pony. "I can practically carry him over to that bucket."

"Sue-Lee and Peter are tied at fifty points each, with Dale only five points behind. Whoever wins this challenge will win the contest and the grand prize trophy."

We eyed each other up with grins, like competitors on the battlefield.

"Everyone ready, then?" Hawk said. "Go!"

We each trotted over to our designated ponies. My pony was a pudgy black one that looked half asleep. Tentatively taking hold of the halter, I murmured a few soft words to the pony, doing my best to act like that guy in *The Horse Whisperer*. From behind me, I suddenly heard a whinny and some stamping of hooves. Dale was heaving on his lead rope, trying to muscle his horse toward the gate, but his pony would have none of it.

At the other side of the enclosure, I noticed that Sue-Lee—ever the quick thinker—had reached through the fence and plucked a handful of green grass and hay that was growing beside a post. Unfortunately, her strategy was not working either, as her pony sniffed it and turned his nose up at her offering. Perhaps he was waiting for exquisite sugar cubes and glazed carrots.

Of course! That was it! Carrots. I knew it would take a few minutes to fetch a couple of carrots from the Billy Brine's restaurant a half block away, but I had a hunch that it was worth trying. I dropped the rope, and ran out the paddock gate toward the promenade.

"Where are you going?" hollered Hawk after me.

"I'll be back in a sec," I yelled over my shoulder.

All my years of jogging served me well as I sprinted down the sidewalk. Inside the restaurant, I slapped a five dollar bill on the counter and quickly made my request. They looked at me a bit oddly, but complied. Within a minute I was back out the door and running for the paddock. I had been gone for no longer than four minutes.

Hawk grinned when he saw the orange carrots protruding from my hand, and he told me to get busy. I saw Sue-Lee's pony now following her around the well-trodden path of the enclosure but making no move toward the gate. I shoved a carrot in front of my pony, and he eagerly began munching on it. The brakes came off, and the horse plodded forward out the gate with me in the lead.

Dale, who was still tugging on his rope and yelling at his horse, saw what I was doing with the carrot and began crowing "No fair." A smug sense of self-satisfaction came over me. I knew I had the contest wrapped up. I knew that my pony would follow me right out the gate, along the beach, through the ditch, and over to the water pail. The plan was perfect.

My pony, however, disagreed.

Once the first carrot had disappeared, the pony stopped cold. The second carrot I put in front of him met with a blank, indifferent stare. I took a sugar cube from my pocket and waved it in front of the horse's mouth. No interest whatsoever.

At that moment, I saw Sue-Lee quietly leading her horse past me. She was using no carrots, no hay, and no brute strength or strong language. I suddenly understood why she had been leading the pony around the well-worn circular path in the paddock: she had taken the extra time to gain the horse's trust and to 'get to know' it.

Sure enough, the contest was over within seconds. We stood watching as her pony dipped its head to the water pail and drank. After the horses were back in the enclosure, we thanked the attendant and gathered on the beach to congratulate Sue-Lee. She had won the contest fair and square.

A pharmaceutical company recognizing the huge part-time labor pool that would be developing as more and more baby boomers retired established an internal temporary staffing function where retiring employees could register, indicating what type of projects they would be interested in, how much time they could dedicate, and what their general availability would be. The model was so successful that they opened up the practice to retirees from other companies and made available the part-time labor pool to strategic partners, vendors, and customers.

"What is the lesson from this last challenge?" asked Hawk, after we gathered in a circle on the sand.

"Simple," said Dale. "Don't have a jackass on the end of the rope."

"Are you referring to the horse or you?" quipped Sue-Lee.

"The lesson is, get to know your candidate first," I offered.

"Yes, and make concessions, too," said Hawk. "Adapt, be flexible, try different things. Be prepared to go out of your way to find the carrots and sugar cubes, if that's what they want."

"I tried that," I said. "It didn't work."

He held up a finger of caution. "What didn't work for one candidate might have worked for another. Or it might have worked on a different day or month, depending on what's going on in the candidate's life at that particular time."

We started walking back along the sidewalk toward the bonfires at the end of the main street. "We have spent a lot of time talking about concessions and being flexible on what you *offer* new hires," Hawk continued. "Now, the other part of concession planning is being more flexible about the types of people you hire."

"What do you mean?" Dale asked, scratching a mosquito bite on his arm. "You're saying we should settle for candidates who aren't that good?"

"I mean, you should know the job inside out and thoroughly understand who can and cannot do the job. Too often hiring managers have blinders on when they start trying to fill a position, and they frequently overlook talented people. For instance, this yard work job that you were recruiting for this morning ... let's evaluate the type of person you tried to recruit."

Dale groaned. "It was a waste of time. Apart from the two teens we found, there are no kids in that town who are going to take a crappy job doing yard work for two days."

Hawk held up a warning finger. "First of all, it's not a crappy job to the right person. For the right candidate, it might be just what they're looking for. Second, I never, ever said you should look for teenagers. I said you should approach *people*. I even used the words *whippersnappers* and *go-getters* didn't I? You were the ones who assumed I meant young people, because that's who you thought would be most likely to do the yard work. And you'd be right. They would be *most likely*. But they're not the only ones who would do it."

I almost slapped myself on the forehead. Tommy's grandmother! "I met someone I should have asked," I said. "But I highly doubt she would have been interested. She said she had a few functions this weekend."

Hawk scoffed. "Functions?! I know what kind of functions they go to. It's ladies' teas and swap meets and things like that."

"How would you know? Your girlfriend go to those things?" said Dale with a grin.

"The point is," said Hawk, ignoring Dale's comment, "if you find you're coming up short, look outside the box. Change the parameters of your job description if need be, as long as it doesn't compromise the quality of the job output."

"So, you're saying we should have asked senior citizens?" said Dale. "I can't start hiring seniors to do heavy construction jobs."

"Maybe not seniors," said Hawk. "But what about the semi-retired … people in their fifties? Mature workers can be a gold mine for all of you. They'll work part-time or on contract, they won't take as many sick days or as many days off to tend to kids. They won't get involved in office politics, or if they do it will probably be in a positive manner. They can be incredibly loyal. These people are your best friends."

At a break in the wall at the end of Main Street, Hawk stopped and told us there would be fewer mosquitoes down near one of the bonfires. He led us down some steps onto the sandy beach. We strolled over to the water's edge where I admired the shimmering moonlight reflected off the water. Thirty yards to our left a huge bonfire crackled and snapped, and I could feel the heat even from this distance. Beyond the flames, I saw some teenagers planting some cylindrical objects in the sand. Fireworks, I guessed.

Sue-Lee spoke up. "You're saying that we should be hiring older staff, not only because we have to in order to get the work done, but because it can be a very smart business decision? It can be good for morale and productivity?"

"You got it," Hawk smiled at her.

"And we should change our structure so that they can work flex hours?" Sue-Lee bit her lip. "I can't have half my senior staff cutting back to part-time. It would be a scheduling nightmare, not to mention coordinating pension and benefits and stuff."

"Most of those people will willingly forego pension and benefits."

"I don't know...."

"It would be worth it," Hawk said calmly. "You will retain many of them who would normally quit outright. Plus, you'll attract new, talented people from other companies that are not offering flex hours."

Hawk stared at us for a moment to let the thought sink in. Then he went on. "But now think about this: it won't be exclusively the mature workers voluntarily looking for part-time hours. It'll be anyone who decides they want some flexibility and doesn't want to be tied down. It could be someone who wants to travel more, or stay home more—like a new mom—or someone who wants to go back to school part time, or someone who wants to try working in a different industry altogether."

"I don't know about that," I said skeptically. "Our economy is set up for people working full time jobs. Flex schedules have been tried in the past, but it never seems to take hold."

"Yeah," Dale agreed. "I can buy into your other predictions, but I'm not sure how much room I've got left in my basket for this theory of yours."

Hawk laughed. "*My* theory? It's hardly mine. Analysts everywhere are predicting this. Even back in the late nineties, in his book *Boom, Bust & Echo*, David Foot wrote that the time has come for a flexible workforce. But Foot also said that managers can't quite accept that part-time workers are committed workers."

> Procter & Gamble and Eli Lilly formed a partnership that will serve as a "job board" for hiring retired employees. This partnership was formed in anticipation of the coming retirement boom. Companies that participate in the partnership will be able to access thousands of retired and semi retired people for part-time and contract work.

"What about mandatory retirement at age 65?" Sue-Lee asked.

"Gone," said Hawk. "The massive numbers of baby boomers will put adequate pressure on the government to remove that. Remember, there are 10 million baby boomers in our workforce. We can't afford to have all of them drop off the payroll and start collecting full pensions."

"I heard talk of them changing the pension system, too," I said.

Hawk nodded. "Another thing the government will probably have to change. They'll need to modify the system so that part-time workers can draw a partial pension … something you can't do right now if you're working at all."

"You should run for office," joked Dale. "Sounds like we need an overhaul of our labor policies."

"Oh, wait, there's more," smiled Hawk. "Consider this: companies have been offshoring more and more jobs because of the cheap, readily available workers overseas. What if, instead of offshoring, companies were able to bring in cheap foreign workers to our country?"

"So you think that our immigration laws have to be relaxed?" asked Dale.

"There are many talented workers outside our borders who would love a chance to work here, so why not go after them? Let's keep the work here, and have those people paying taxes and spending their income locally. I've read quite a few startling figures on immigration lately. One said that, by 2050, the U.S. population is expected to increase by 50%, and half of the population will be from what we now call 'minority' groups."

"Half the population?" exclaimed Sue-Lee. "Hiring and managing diverse people will be a major issue for quite some time."

I exhaled, almost as if I'd been punched in the gut. "I guess our workplace is dynamic and in the future it is going to look a whole lot different."

Dale added, "And we're going to have to start hiring people we might not have considered as readily in the past—like those mature workers."

Hawk nodded. "But be careful. I don't mean that you should lower your standards because of the shortage of talent. Be flexible, not foolish. Compromising doesn't mean you should cut corners in hiring. Don't hire people who either can't do the job or won't flourish in the job."

"But having a warm body doing something," I said, "can sometimes be better than nothing at all getting done."

"Not always," said Sue-Lee. "The quality of work can go down. In accounting we can't take the chance of an audit being done improperly. We have liability issues."

"So do we in construction," added Dale. "We're in trouble if we build something wrong."

"I'm not talking about the high level jobs," I said. "More like the unskilled labor positions."

"You all have valid points," said Hawk. "Quality issues will be huge, depending on the type of work being done. So that's *one* reason why companies should not cut corners when hiring. Bad hires can cost companies millions. Are there any other reasons?"

"What about training time?" Sue-Lee said. "It obviously costs more to train someone who is unqualified. And it pulls other staff away from what they should be focusing on."

"Absolutely," agreed Hawk.

"And they require more supervision once they're up and running, too," added Sue-Lee, now on a roll. "Plus, the morale of the other staff can deteriorate if the underqualified employees are dragging things down."

"What about accidents?" piped up Dale. "We have more down time because they make more mistakes, both at the planning stage and on the actual construction site. Plus, the mistakes often mean more wasted materials because they don't know what they're doing."

"So, efficiencies decrease and production costs rise?" summarized Hawk.

We all nodded. I thought about some of the young software designers my company had hired lately. One of them had made a mistake in the coding for a new product. Had we not caught the error, it would have cost the company millions of dollars.

"So it's crucial not to compromise too much when hiring," noted Hawk. "In the book *Good to Great,* Collins observed that the leaders of great companies seemed to follow this motto: 'When in doubt, don't hire—keep looking.'"

In the distance, we saw two teens attempting to light several fireworks on the beach.

"So, does everyone understand the importance of concession planning and periodic change?" Hawk asked. "And the importance of building it into your recruiting plan?"

"I think we're probably all convinced by now," said Dale, just as one of the teenagers got a small flame going at the end of one of the fireworks.

"Are you really?" asked Hawk. "There is one huge concession that I haven't touched on yet, which you may be forced to make, like it or not."

After a lead-in like that, he of course had our attention. "What is it?" I asked.

Just then a high-pitched whistling sound filled the air, followed by the boom of the fireworks exploding high overhead. A beautiful green and red starburst filled the sky.

Hawk looked at Sue-Lee again. "I want to ask you a question. Last night, Sue-Lee, I asked you if you were willing to do *anything* for the company, and you said, yes, that you had been for twenty years."

"Twenty-five," she corrected him.

A second set of fireworks exploded, and the kids shouted and clapped at their success.

"Let me ask you this, then. Are you willing to take a pay decrease of thirty percent for the next ten years, until retirement?"

Sue-Lee looked around at the rest of us, then back at Hawk. "Of course not. Why should we do that? We worked hard to get where we're at."

"I didn't ask the group that question, I asked you. Are *you* prepared to take that decrease?"

She stood quietly for a moment, then folded her arms across her chest. "No, I'm not. Why are you asking just me?"

"I can see you're getting defensive," Hawk replied with a grin. "You've told me that you can't find junior accountants because they're sick and tired of low pay, long hours, pressure from clients, business development expectations, and the sense that they're never working on their own company's books. There are a few things in there you can't change, because they're inherent to the job. But what if you focused on two things to improve? What if you paid staff more, and what if you hired more of them so that the workload wasn't so heavy and the hours were more attractive?"

"That's unfeasible. We wouldn't survive as a firm."

Hawk raised his eyebrows as if to say, *Are you sure?*

"Of course you'd survive," I jumped in. "You'd just have less profit for the partners."

"Perhaps thirty percent less?" offered Dale mischievously.

"Sue-Lee, I have a pretty good idea what you're making," Hawk said to her earnestly. "And if we take thirty percent off your comp package, it would still leave a very, very healthy income, wouldn't it?"

"What I make is beside the point," she retorted, as more fireworks boomed overhead.

"No, it's not. It's very much part of the point. Within the new economy, you're viewed by the lower level workers as one of the fat cats."

With a clenched jaw, Sue-Lee stared at the smoke-filled sky, her eyes smoldering with indignation. "How dare you," she said. "I've worked hard all my life. I've put in my time and I don't feel guilty about being remunerated nicely. So don't lecture me about what I should do."

To this point of the weekend, Hawk had been rather happy-go-lucky and genteel. Now, in the light of the bonfire, I saw a different look in his eye, a look that at once both pitied and condemned. Suddenly the words were churning from his mouth. "So many of you high-level managers are the same. You have this sense of entitlement, that you worked hard and put in your time for twenty-five years, therefore everyone below you should suck it up and do the same. You swell with pride about your companies and, over rounds of single malt scotch and cigars, you brag about your latest corporate earnings or stock split."

A cold silence had descended on us. It seemed as though even the bonfire had stopped crackling for a moment, in anticipation of what was to come.

"And you people," continued Hawk, "you talented individuals with the vision to lead armies of workers, will be the quickest to fall in the new economy. Why? Because so many of you have risen to the top on confidence and ego, and you think that *everyone* should want to work at your company, and that every prospective employee should thank you for the chance to do so. I'm trying to tell you what you need to do, what kind of mind shift is required, and you don't want to hear it, because you're not hearing what you like."

Hawk kicked an empty soda can. "And you sure as hell don't know how to be gracious. Many of you don't know how to swallow your pride and admit that you need help. If you're like this with *me*, I can't imagine the image you project to a potential hire sitting across from you in an interview. You probably sit and look at that little twerp with the shaved head and tattoos sitting across from you and say to yourselves, 'How dare he spend his time grilling *me* about the perqs of the job.' Well, guess what? That little twerp just could be the saving grace for your company. Instead, that twerp will go across town and land a job with a competitor who doesn't let pride get in the way. You'll be left puzzled, thinking, 'I had the best carrots and the sweetest hay and the finest spring water. And, hey, I even put the water in a shiny new stainless steel pail. What more could he ask for? Why didn't he drink, damn it?"

We stood in silence for a while, embarrassed and uncomfortable at what Hawk was saying.

Finally, it was Sue-Lee who broke the ice. "This mind shift you're talking about … that's what this whole boot camp is about. You're telling us the old way of thinking is dead."

"We need an attitude adjustment," I added. "We have to set our pride aside."

Hawk just nodded and stood quietly gazing across the lake, as if he were scanning the darkness for something.

"Well," said Dale finally, "if pride goeth before a fall, then I suppose I'm due for a major tumble."

Sue-Lee and I turned to stare at him. We had never heard Dale use a famous quote in his entire life.

"What?" Dale said defensively. "I learned that from a fortune cookie at a Chinese food joint the other day."

We heard Hawk chuckle, and the mood suddenly seemed lighter. He turned to Sue-Lee. "I apologize if I seem rude, but I feel strongly about this new hiring landscape. And keep in mind," he said, as he addressed Dale and me, "I have only used Sue-Lee as an example. You will all be faced with this situation."

Dale let out a sigh. "Let me get this straight. You think us top dogs are going to have to take more from our bottom line and give it to the employees in order to attract them."

"To attract them … and to *keep* them," nodded Hawk. "Right now in business schools they teach you that a company's expense column should allow anywhere from 30% to 50% for employee wages, depending on the industry. I foresee that this will climb sharply very soon. Perhaps as high as 60% to 70% for some companies in the future."

"That's just great," snorted Dale, still trying to keep the mood light. "We entrepreneurs take all the risk building up companies, but now our profits are going to shrink, is that what you're saying?"

"That's what I'm saying."

An uncomfortable laugh escaped me. "Oh, so now we're talking social-ism again?"

"Not at all. On the contrary, this scenario will have more to do with capitalism than socialism. In a free market economy, it's all about supply and demand. Supply of talent will be acutely short, and demand will be acutely high. The best bidders will secure the commodity—in this case, the best workers."

"You said the *best* bidders, not the *highest* bidders."

"That's right. In some cases it will be the highest bidders—in other words, the ones with the deepest pockets. But more often than not, it will be the companies that provide the best overall package. Along with remu-neration, that may also involve the other things we talked about: flex hours, increased vacation time, special in-house amenities—you name it. But there's no question, wages for entry level positions will rise in order to attract workers."

"What do you mean 'rise'?" asked Sue-Lee. "What kind of increase are we talking about?"

Hawk shrugged. "Where you once were paying junior accountants thirty-five thousand dollars a year, you'll now have to pay them fifty thousand. Where Dale once saw his laborers making ten or twelve dollars an hour, they'll probably be commanding twice that by 2020. Companies will try to pass the increased cost of business along to the customer in terms of higher prices, but they won't be able to get away with transfer-ring it all."

Dale winced. "So, if this whole thing is going to severely cut into com-pany profits, do you think the stock market will go down?" asked Dale. "After all, if corporate profits are down, stock prices will fall. And if stock prices fall, people will sell off stocks like crazy."

"I'm not an expert in that area, so I can't say for sure," said Hawk. "Nor can I say if increased prices will translate into inflation and higher interest rates. I just don't know. All I know is that employee wages will be going up in order to attract and retain staff."

We sat in silence for a while, the only sound being the low crackle of the fire. I thought once more about the book I had read, *Impending Crisis*. It warned that few executives really comprehended the risk that the labor shortage will cause to their bottom line. In general, bond ratings could drop and stock prices tumble, threatening capitalization.

"Time to call it a night," Hawk said. He pointed at our motel two blocks away along the shore. "You might as well head back and get some sleep. Let's agree to meet for breakfast tomorrow morning and we'll wrap things up before you go back to the city. I'll pick you up at nine."

"Are we finally going to get to the recruiting plan?" I asked.

Hawk smiled. "Yes, we'll finally cover that."

We said our goodnights and Hawk crossed the street and made his way to the parking lot and his SUV. Dale, Sue-Lee and I began walking along the beachfront sidewalk. The pathway ahead seemed slightly empty and it felt odd to be alone without Hawk, who had clearly done most of the talking in the past twenty-four hours. None of us spoke as we walked and contemplated Hawk's lecture. The only noise I remember hearing was a duck calling from the lake—a lonely sound in the dark distance.

* * * * *

Chapter 11—Manager Action Steps

Some suggested actions for proactive managers include:

- ✓ **Concession planning**—In a dynamic and fast-changing world you must insist that every program and process be "flexible" to meet the changing expectations of candidates. Being flexible starts with shifting your recruiting strategy as the economy and the power relationship between candidates and the employer change.
- ✓ **Be flexible**—Learn to prioritize candidates based on their desirability. Be more flexible with candidates that are in higher demand. Make it a primary goal of your recruiting process to find or develop "*the* job" that top candidates are seeking. Have the flexibility to customize an opportunity so that it fits *their* needs. Remember, the leaders with the best talent will win.
- ✓ **Prepare for changing expectations**—Change your traditional mindset when hiring is coming up short. Accept that the current workforce is diverse, aging, and interested in work/life balance. Calculate the costs of low quality or bad hires at your firm. Change the parameters of your job description to be flexible with things that are important to candidates. But be careful about lowering standards just because talent is scarce.
- ✓ **Continuous improvement**—Because the world of recruiting will become more competitive, it is essential that every program and process include a feedback mechanism and contain a continuous-improvement element.
- ✓ **Consider strategic alternatives**—Forecast future needs and make the necessary changes to your recruiting tools to meet the needs. And in particular, make sure your recruiting sources reach the global candidate pool. Also consider offshoring and outsourcing as opportunities to cut labor costs if you excel at international recruiting and retention. In addition, be prepared to increase salaries, based on performance, as the demand for top talent increases.
- ✓ **Poaching is an alternative**—Even when there is a labor shortage, *you* won't have a shortage if you excel at poaching away talent from your competitors and in blocking them from stealing your best. You can find hundreds of well-trained and up-to-date top performers if you have the courage to look at your competitors. Recruiting is Sales, so compete for talent like you would compete against your competition for customers.

CHAPTER 12

The Battle Plan: Your Recruiting Strategy

> *Chapter 12 Learning Goals:*
>
> > 1. Learn the final strategy for developing a recruitment plan.

*"Plans are only good intentions unless they immediately
degenerate into hard work."*
*"Unless commitment is made, there are only promises
and hopes ... but no plans."*
(Peter Drucker)

It was Sunday morning, our final hours with Hawk. We were gathered for our farewell brunch at the Billy Brine's restaurant where I had bought the carrots and sugar cubes the night before. The restaurant was packed with well-heeled diners sipping their Mimosas and lattes, while it sounded like Diana Krall was tinkling lightly on a piano somewhere amongst the fishing nets strung throughout the open beam ceiling. We were seated in a quiet corner booth with an expansive window overlooking the lake.

Our waiter, a polite, acne-riddled kid of about twenty, set an easel and chalkboard beside our table and went through the brunch specials handwritten there. We placed our orders and sat back sipping our coffees, admiring the brilliant blue skyline above the lake.

We had just finished a cup of fresh fruit and yogurt, and were waiting for the main entrees when Hawk cleared his throat. "I want to congratulate you. You guys have done well this weekend. Ten of you started out to find me, but only three of you got this far."

I smiled at him. "I think I can speak for the group when I say we've learned a lot. Thanks."

"You're welcome. I'm glad you think it was valuable information," Hawk answered. "But it's only as valuable as you make it. Remember, many managers will say they're committed to the talent principle, but they won't see it through. Through fear or apathy, they won't implement change, either in themselves or in their companies."

"We'll just keep sprinting toward that retirement finish line, right?" Sue-Lee said.

Hawk smiled. "There is one last thing we need to discuss before you head back. It's both a summary of everything you have learned, and a plan for the road ahead."

We waited patiently for him to continue.

"We agree that the war for talent is here," he said. "You're in a battle for top performers, right?"

We nodded.

"So what does your battle plan look like?"

"What do you mean?" I asked.

"If I walked into your office, where would I find your recruiting strategy written down?"

"Aha!" said Sue-Lee, across from me in the booth. "We finally get to the recruiting strategy."

This drew a laugh from Hawk.

> Every year a capital equipment manufacturer with locations in seven countries dedicates the entire month of October to strategic business and product lifecycle planning. Every employee from top to bottom is consumed with analyzing successes, failures, and projections for the future. Recently the firm added an extra layer of analysis to the massive process. All managers must now report how changes in strategy and product lifecycle will alter the firm's talent needs, and on what timeline. This new layer to the process produces a forecast for the recruiting function so that hard to fill jobs can be sourced *prior* to requisitions being created.

"Yes, we're finally here. So, I ask you again, what does your recruiting strategy look like?"

Dale spoke up beside me. "My company doesn't have one."

"Neither do we," I said.

"Don't feel bad. Most companies don't," replied Hawk. "Up 'til now, if you had a job opening, only then did the wheels of recruitment start turning in order to fill it. Today, those wheels continuously need to be turning. *Continuously.* Don't wait until there's a round hole and then start looking for a round peg to fill it. Starting tomorrow when you get back to your offices, spend a few days or weeks developing a recruiting plan."

"A few weeks? That's a little excessive," I commented.

Hawk stuck his finger in the air. "Every year, you managers consume yourselves for weeks working on the budget or marketing plan, but most of you don't have a recruitment and retention plan in place. Without great people, your budget and marketing plan mean nothing."

"*Everything* starts with great people," Sue-Lee nodded thoughtfully. "That's one of the key points you keep telling us."

"Right," Hawk said. "It's an important point you'll see over and over in business articles and books these days. I think it's summarized best in *Good to Great*, where Jim Collins says, 'First Who … then What.'"

"I don't know that I'll be able to convince my bosses that we need to create a recruiting strategy," I muttered.

"If they're committed to creating an organization that values top talent, they'll have to," Hawk replied. "Tell them it's like renovating a house. It's much less efficient when you don't plan. For instance, is it cheaper to call in a plumber once for the bathroom, and then again for the kitchen, and again for the laundry area, or get him to come and do it all at once? Or, what happens if you make a mistake and drywall before you plan where your electrical or plumbing has to come out? It will cost you money. The bottom line is, plan ahead, save time and money, and get what you want the first time."

"I can relate to that," Dale said. "I like it. I just have to get my managers thinking that way."

"Remember, it's a shift in mindset and it won't be easy, but it will be vital. They'll have to adopt what's called the talent management perspective."

"What's that?" I asked.

"It's a term that means you go beyond simply adding bodies, to the mindset of how you can best handle the staffing process in order to maximize overall productivity. I think it's summed up best by a fellow named David Creelman of Creelman Research. He preaches that when a company starts thinking this way, then all issues are seen from the perspective of 'How will this affect our critical talent?' or 'What role does talent play in this issue?'"

"Can you give us an example?" Dale asked.

"Well, traditionally, the HR view is that health benefits are all about being 'good' to people. Creelman says that in the talent management perspective, benefits are about attracting and retaining talent."

We sat absorbing this for a moment before Dale spoke up. "So back to the plan. I know how the budgeting process works, but what goes into a recruiting plan, Hawk?"

"Well, keep in mind what we said before, that the top talent will be like customers, and you'll be selling to them. Therefore, you can look at a recruiting plan like a marketing plan. So what would you do when building a marketing plan?" He looked at me.

I cleared my throat. "First, figure out your niche and what your target market is. Second, analyze customers and assess their needs. Third, define how you're going to position and brand your product with a unique selling proposition—in other words, what you have to offer that others don't."

"Go on," Hawk said.

"Fourth, establish channels to reach customers, and the methods used to reach them. Fifth, determine your goals and targets. Sixth, assign responsibilities so that people are accountable. Oh, and, last, monitor and evaluate results."

"Excellent," applauded Hawk. "You'll find different views on exactly what goes into a marketing plan, but most of them loosely encompass those seven key points. Setting recruiting strategy is very similar."

We heard Dale let out a sigh. "I'm not a marketing guy. I don't know how I'm going to remember this," he complained. "I need something concrete I can take back with me."

Hawk reached for the restaurant's easel and chalkboard and pulled it beside his bench seat. With a napkin he erased the entire board, then took up the chalk and began writing. He told Dale to grab a napkin and pen and copy everything down.

Our server arrived with more coffee. He glanced at the chalkboard and saw what Hawk was writing there. Rather than seeming perturbed that his work had been erased, the waiter backed away, puzzled, as if he hadn't been informed about the new daily specials.

"Voila. Here's my recruiting strategy," said Hawk, pointing at the chalkboard. "It's based on the marketing plan we just talked about. I have mixed up the order a bit, but the result is the same."

We looked at the board. He had written at the top, 'Hawk's Recruiting Strategy of Mixed Metaphors' and underneath that:

- (responsibilities)—You Are All Headhunters
- (channels)—Stop Fishing in the Wrong Places
- (target market/niche)—Who'll Take Your Bait?
- (customer analysis)—How Do They Take Their Coffee?
- (customer needs assessment)—Look Out for the Career Chasm
- (product positioning/branding/USP)—From Maybe to Yes
- (goals/targets)—Ready, Aim …
- (evaluation)—Weigh & Measure Your Catch
- (feedback loop)—Concession Planning

The three of us studied the words on the chalkboard. The recruiting plan seemed familiar.

"Remember," Hawk said, "this is not meant to teach you how to become a corporate recruiter, but only how to *think* like a headhunter when going after the candidate. And we've agreed that the candidate is the new customer."

I kept staring at the chalkboard. All of a sudden I realized that Hawk's recruiting strategy was *very* familiar to me indeed. In fact, we had been living it for the last two days. With all the lectures and challenges, Hawk had put us through the motions of a real, live recruiting plan. Before I could speak up, Sue-Lee started laughing. She had obviously figured it out, as well.

Dale was the last to get it. "You shrewd fox," he said to Hawk. "You brought it to life for us. Your boot camp walked us through the entire plan. You knew that's how we'd remember it best."

Hawk smiled. "Not just remember it best, but actually see the importance of each step. If you didn't believe this stuff worked, you would have never changed your ways."

Our main dishes arrived and we hungrily set to work on them. My poached eggs were perfectly done, and I noticed that Dale had a mountain of pancakes to go with his sausages. Across from me, Sue-Lee's blueberry crepes looked delicious, while Hawk had a simple order of whole-grain toast in front of him.

"This trip was worthwhile," Dale said to Hawk. "Thanks for your guidance."

"Yes, it was useful," I agreed. "I can see myself implementing these ideas."

"It was kind of fun, too," Sue-Lee said. I could tell she was swallowing a bit of pride by admitting it.

"Which reminds me," said Hawk to her. "You win the contest."

She grinned. "What's the prize?"

"Yeah, you said it was a trophy of some sort," added Dale enthusiastically.

Hawk dug into a large plastic bag on the floor. He pulled out what looked like a toy, but then I saw it was one of those talking fishes mounted on a board. He flicked a switch and the fish started flopping robotically, while the music and lyrics to the song *Don't Worry, Be Happy* started playing. We all started laughing, and people at nearby tables smiled, as Sue-Lee, embarrassed, accepted the fish.

"There's your trophy fish. Nice catch," said Hawk. "Actually, all three of you should take the lyrics to heart. You could stand to relax a little more."

We chatted as we ate, and I brought up the topic of Hawk's consulting fee for the boot camp. He smiled and explained that he wanted us each to make a charitable donation to the cancer society in memory of his wife. "That's all you have to do," he said. "Then the slate is clean. Camp Hee-Ho-Head-Hunt-Ha has come to an end."

"Hey, what about all the work left at your cottage?" Dale asked. "We never got those jobs finished."

"Oh, there's really not much to do," Hawk replied. "Things like cleaning the eaves, painting the dock. I can find some people to help finish things off."

"These days it seems like everyone is short staffed, including you," I said, somewhat apologetically.

"That brings up a good point," Hawk said. He sat back and thought for a moment. "What if I called each of your spouses and told them that, because you didn't recruit enough staff to fix up the place, that you had to stay and finish those jobs yourself?"

Dale laughed. "I think that before you could blink you'd find me in the car getting out of Dodge."

"I had a feeling you'd say that," Hawk answered with a grin. "But keep what you just said in mind. It's reflective of where our economy is headed. There is going to be increased pressure on existing staff to pick up the extra slack … to become more productive, especially the managers."

I spoke up. "Hawk, I hear what you're saying, but isn't our workforce more productive now than ever before?"

"True," replied Hawk. "We have steadily become more productive over the last half century. At the end of the second World War, the North American economy was eight times smaller than it is today, but the number of workers back then was only half what it is today."

Sue-Lee's accounting mind snapped into high gear. "So you're saying we're four times as productive today as back then?"

"That's right," replied Hawk, as he spread some orange marmalade on his toast. "Some of that is clearly due to machinery and computers and automation. But some of it is due to increased individual workload. That engagement study I mentioned reported that the average person is spending more hours per week on the job."

"Maybe that's why there's so much more talk about job-related stress?" I offered.

"Yes, that same study said high job stress is twice as prevalent as it was ten years ago," said Hawk. "We have to ask ourselves how much more productive we can become. When the impending reduction of workers comes along, the only way to maintain overall productivity levels—never mind grow those levels—will be to increase productivity per worker."

"So even more stress?" said Sue-Lee.

"And more staff turnover?" I offered.

Hawk bit into his toast, and his silence answered for him.

"Well, I can't afford to lose more people," said Dale. "I'm going to make recruiting my number one priority when I get back."

"How about you, Hawk?" Sue-Lee said. "Are you going to make it a top priority to find people for your chores around the cottage?"

We looked at her and saw a twinkle in her eye, but none of us seemed to know where she was going with the conversation.

"Let me use one of your *if-then* statements," Sue-Lee said mischievously. "*If* I found someone who could handle some of the odd jobs at your cottage, *then* would you accept that help?"

"Of course," responded Hawk.

"Good," Sue-Lee grinned. "Because I have your new helper lined up."

"Who is it?"

"Oh, you know her well."

Hawk stared back at her. "Not Gladys?"

Sue-Lee nodded. "You said there were no restrictions on who could do the job. You wanted a 'whippersnapper' so I found you one."

At that moment, as if on cue, Gladys entered the restaurant and walked toward our table, smiling and waving at various people she knew along the way. With her radiant smile and pretty, petite figure, she seemed to light up the room as she moved toward us. "Hello, hello, good morning," she beamed at us. Before anyone could respond, she promptly slid her bottom into the booth beside Hawk, creating a nice, tight fit with him. "Well," she said to him with a twinkle in her eye, "I hear you might need me back at the cottage. So where do we begin?"

Sue-Lee, Dale, and I couldn't stop grinning at Hawk.

Now, Camp Hee-Ho-Head-Hunt-Ha had come to an end.

* * * * *

Chapter 12—Manager Action Steps

Some suggested actions for proactive managers include:

✓ **Be customer centric**—Make recruiting your number one priority because, if you don't, both you and your organization will suffer. Develop a written recruiting plan that is customer centric. Develop your recruiting plan like a marketing plan. Include:
- (Responsibilities)—You Are All Headhunters
- (Channels)—Quit Fishing in the Wrong Places
- (Target market/niche)—Stop Using the Wrong Bait
- (Customer analysis)—How Do They Take Their Coffee?
- (Customer needs assessment)—Look Out for the Career Chasm
- (Product positioning/branding/USP)—From Maybe to Yes
- (Goals/targets)—Ready, Aim ...
- (Evaluation)—Weigh & Measure Your Catch
- (Feedback loop)—Concession Planning

✓ **Think and act outside the box**—Begin to think out of the box to find new ways to adapt your recruiting to the changing workforce and world of work.

✓ **Improve productivity**—Periodically measure your workforce productivity by comparing the ratio that is generated when you divide the number of employees into the firm's total revenue. Try to improve that revenue-per-employee ratio through great hiring and retention. Develop actions that attract and retain top employees with the goal of maximizing overall company productivity.

EPILOGUE

"Courage and perseverance have a magical talisman,
before which difficulties disappear and obstacles vanish into air."
(John Quincy Adams)

I think back to that weekend last summer, and to the long, silent drive home on Sunday afternoon during which we sat silently staring at the long road before us, leading us back to our demanding jobs and busy family lives. I remember sitting and reflecting on all that P.D. Hawkston had said, and, while I wasn't certain, I think Sue-Lee and Dale both felt the same as I: full of apprehension, but mostly excited that we were better armed to win the war for talent ahead.

Six months later the three of us had noticed several positive changes in our organizations' recruiting efforts. Fighting against complacency and outright opposition within our companies, we had persevered and implemented recruiting strategies that were working really well. At my software company, we started identifying top performers and had already hired two people, without actual roles to fill. Sure enough, they had found niches quickly and were providing enormous value already. At Dale's company, he had all his managers start rating employees, and then release bad ones, pay attention to—and even hug—the good ones, and give the concessions the stars needed to be productive. At Sue-Lee's firm, the partners were initially reluctant to start thinking of candidates as customers, but they were doing their best to develop a unique selling proposition, a better employment brand, and an initiative to market their corporate culture differently than the other large accounting firms in town.

One day over breakfast, the three of us had gathered with the other members of our networking group and tried to explain what we had learned from Hawk. Although we had encouraged them to seek out Hawk for themselves, they seemed reluctant. "He sounds like a crackpot," was one friend's comment, which met with laughter from the group. "I don't want to go all that way just to haul logs over a ravine," said another. "Can't you just recommend a book or something?"

For no other reason than to say hello, I had tried contacting Hawk a half-dozen times via telephone, but there was never any answer. Whenever I called, I got his answering machine with the abrupt message, 'It's Hawk. Leave a message. I'm probably out fishing right now. You should be, too.' I liked his recording. Short and to-the-point. Each time I heard it, I hung up without leaving a message, but it was somehow reassuring to hear his voice each time, knowing that he was out there somewhere and that his message was always there when I needed it. He had done his job. He inspired us. He gave us tools and direction. He never spoiled us by giving us a fish. Hawk lived the old proverb: "Give a man a fish and you feed him for a day. Teach a man to fish and you feed him for a lifetime."

—END—

APPENDIX

Each chapter throughout this book has introduced new concepts that build on one another to reposition recruiting as a strategic-level management activity. Hopefully you have leveraged the learnings of Peter, Dale, and Sue-Lee along with the action steps presented at the end of each chapter to mentally retool your own approach. To further support your efforts to catch the best talent the market has to offer, we have assembled a number of simple tools, checklists, and information sources that may assist you in your efforts.

Checklist: Preparing for the War for Talent

The basic steps in preparing your recruiting effort for the war for talent include:

☑ Written Recruitment Strategy
Your strategy must include new, aggressive strategies, approaches, and tools. If you want to win the war for talent, you must include "guerilla warfare" tactics that your competition can't or won't use.

☑ Accountability and Rewards
Rewards are an essential part of getting people to pay attention to great recruiting, so make them an integral part of the recruiting plan.

☑ Forecasting and Workforce Planning
You can't have excellence in recruiting without excellent workforce planning. Start by forecasting future needs.

☑ Market Research and Sourcing
The next most significant factor in successful recruiting is great sourcing. Make sure you have processes for identifying and utilizing sources that produce the best on-the-job performers.

☑ Unique Sales Proposition/Employment Brand
The best long-term approach for building a continuous pipeline of quality candidates is to build a strong employment brand. Since the process of building or rebuilding a brand takes time, it is important to make building a brand an early step in your recruiting plan. It is essential that recruiting works closely with other business functions to produce a coordinated effort.

☑ Improving Recruiting Metrics and the Business Case
The cornerstone of any great recruiting effort is utilizing metrics to continually improve everything you do. It is essential to focus on the right metrics from the start.

☑ Feedback Loop

A recruitment strategy should be flexible in order to deal with unforeseen and uncontrollable environmental factors, poor performing new hires and preventable turnover of top-performing employees. Your recruiting efforts can be easily overloaded if your retention effort is weak. Managers must pay attention to both recruiting and retention to minimize preventable turnover.

Understanding the Labor Market

Peter, Dale, and Sue-Lee learned in Chapter 2 that North America will soon face a labor shortage the likes of which have never been encountered before. While a few industries—namely healthcare, technology, and transportation—have already felt the crunch, nearly all industries will be heavily impacted by 2010. It is important to note that for the most part the labor shortage is not attributed to a shortage of people, but rather **a shortage of people with the right skills**.

North America is not the only region of the world facing such a crisis. Nearly every industrialized nation in the world will experience either a decline in the size of the working-age population, or a significantly reduced rate of population growth.

Assembled below is an index of data sources that can help you understand what is going on with the labor market on both the national and local levels. Each of these resources is a valuable source of data that can help you make informed decisions regarding your recruiting and retention strategy.

The Big Picture (Macro Statistics)

To garner an understanding of what is going on around the world with talent, consider the following resources:

- *It's 2008: Do You Know Where Your Talent Is?* This 20-page publication from Deloitte Research delivers an excellent overview of the events and circumstances that are converging to create a worldwide talent crisis. It is available for free as a PDF download at: http://www.deloitte.com/dtt/research/0,1015,sid=26551&cid=71444,00.html.

- **US Department of Labor: Bureau of Labor Statistics**. Packed with enough information to overload your senses, the US Department of Labor makes available through the Bureau of Labor Statistics a myriad of projections on everything from wages by occupation to labor demand by industry. Particular attention should be paid to the sections on "Wages,

Earnings and Benefits," "Demographics," "Employment and Unemployment", and "Industries." The BLS data is available at: http://www.bls.gov/

- **Statistics Canada**. The Canadian counterpart to the US Bureau of Labor Statistics, Statistics Canada can tell you nearly anything about the Canadian Labour Markets. Those interested in the Canadian labour markets should pay attention to the "Labour" and "Population and Demography" subject areas. Statistics Canada is available at: http://www.statcan.ca/start.html.

- **Secretaría del Trabajo y Prevision Social**. The Mexican counterpart to the US Bureau of Labor Statistics, the Secretaría del Trabajo y Prevision Social provides a wealth of labor market statistics under the "Información del Sector" section. The website is provided in Spanish only. Similar statistics are available in English under the International Section of the US Bureau of Labor Statistics site. The Secretaría del Trabajo y Prevision Social is at: http://www.stps.gob.mx/

Your Local Labor Market

Not all municipalities in North America are good about publishing labor market data in a format that is easily accessible, but there are other sources of data that can give you a good indication of current conditions. When it comes to understanding your local labor market, learning about who you compete for talent with is a key concern. The following sources will help you:

- **Major Job Boards**. While not a great source for top caliber talent, such boards are a great place to learn about who you are competing for talent against. Leveraging keyword searches can tell you what firms in your local geography are after the same people. Organizations often become myopic in the view of who they compete against. If domain knowledge can be learned quickly, avoid using it as a filter, opting instead to look at which competitors are after the more difficult-to-acquire knowledge, skills, and abilities. Don't be surprised when you learn just how many firms outside your industry want your

people. Job postings will not only tell you who you are competing against, but also what the relevant demand for such talent
is. This can help you adjust your retention strategies. Major job
boards in North America include:

o   Monster (www.monster.com) (US, Canada, Mexico)

o   CareerBuilder (www.careerbuilder.com) (US, Canada)

o   HotJobs (www.hotjobs.com) (US, Canada, Mexico)

o   Workopolis (www.workopolis.com) (Canada)

- **Local Colleges & Universities**. Enrollment, graduation, and
placement data can be very helpful in determining whether
your recruiting efforts will need to grow in scope outside your
local region due to a shortage in entry level skills production. Most larger schools publish their data online, but smaller
schools may need to be contacted by phone. To find online
enrollment data, leverage the Google search engine at www.
google.com and execute a search with the name of the local
school and the word "enrollment."

- **City-Data.com**. For several years now the folks at City-Data.
com have been aggregating statistical data about US cities
from a multitude of sources. Here you can find local workforce demographic data, stats on the largest employers,
trends related to housing prices and wages, and educational
attainment.

What It All Means For You

While it sounds cliché to say it, knowing about the current condition
of the labor market truly is half the battle. Armed with the facts, you
can predict an array of issues that will help you build a winning team
including:

- Which positions in your organization are most likely to incur increased
turnover as a result of recruiting actions by talent competitors.

- The relative length of time you may have to court top talent
from "date of introduction" through "offer close."

- The bevy of expectations top talent can present and what they can reasonably expect to get.
- The growth in starting salaries that will be required to land even entry-level talent.

This list can go on and on. Just like a product market, the laws of supply and demand govern the labor markets.

How to Craft a Unique Value Proposition

What is a Value Proposition?
In short, a value proposition is a very short offer to an individual (think candidate) or target population (think labor pool) that grants them more value than they give up relative to all of their opportunities (one of which is maintaining the status quo and staying put).

The critical elements involved with crafting a value proposition include:
Understanding your target group, including their values, wants, needs, and the priority they attach to each.

Keep your offer short. If you are lucky, you will get a few sentences (probably two to four) to articulate your value.

Understand that your offer must come out on top in relation to all of the other opportunities at the target's fingertips, one of which is to do nothing.

Identifying candidates' wishes: What they value, want, need ...
In many cases, what they really value is not stated as much as it is implied. To identify the value elements to include in your value proposition, consider the following steps:

- Identify all of the possible elements of value you have to offer, including both tangible and intangible benefits. Be honest. Is it really true that you have the best management team in the industry? How can you prove that, and more importantly how can you disprove your competitors' claim to the same distinction? Only list what you can quickly and easily prove as fact.

- Go through your list and determine which elements are mutually exclusive, that is, more of one requires less of the other. Stock options or grants versus base compensation are usually a good example of that zero-sum situation.

- Rank your elements in terms of a priority assigned to each. You can also use your current employees if they are models you hire against. Test their ranking by putting them through a simulation that requires them to choose more or less of those elements that are mutually exclusive. If the result of this conjoint analysis aligns with their initial ranking, it is probably true.

Crafting your value proposition
A world-class value proposition combines both qualitative and quantitative elements. It uses a mix of financial, emotional, and functional benefits to entice the candidate to act as you desire. Designing the language of the actual proposition is the only thing that makes mastering the art of using value propositions difficult. To accomplish the development of a finely honed and effective value proposition, consider the following:

Start by writing a one-page narrative that clearly puts forth the value your opportunity provides.

Continue cutting your one-page narrative down until you have just two to four sentences that provide the most bang for your buck.

Perform a quality check to make sure your sentences promote value from the target's perspective and use their language.

Lastly, **test** your proposition on a sample from your target audience, and use **their** initial unscripted reaction to fine-tune your message.

How to Find Talent Using a Candidate Behavior Profile

What is a behavioral profile?

One of the basic laws of recruiting is that "A" players know other "A" players. A related law is that the "A" players who don't work for you read, go to, and do the exact same things as your current "A" employees. A behavioral profile is merely a list of the common behaviors (places they hang out, media they use, organizations they join, and events they attend) of top performers in your targeted jobs. By "profiling" the behaviors of your current top performers you can use that information to identify appropriate ways to find and build the interest of other "A" players.

Steps in finding "A" players

- Identify the top performers at your firm who are currently in similar jobs to those you are attempting to fill.

- Tell them how they can help build the team by disclosing (it can be anonymous) "how we would find them" if they were strangers to the firm and the firm was trying to identify them as potential applicants.

- Develop an e-mail questionnaire/checklist. Ask them about their activities. Ask them to specify which issues are most likely to get their attention when they are looking for a job.

Questions for Developing a Behavioral Profile

What should you ask about?
MEDIA

- What papers (and your favorite sections) do you read? How often do you read the classifieds?

- What magazines do you read for pleasure?

- What professional publications and newsletters do you read? Would a job ad get your attention?

- In what chat rooms, listservers, e-mail newsletters, and web pages do you actively participate? In which ones, would a job announcement get your attention?
- To which radio stations do you listen? TV shows?
- What kind of movies and concerts do you enjoy? Where do you attend them?

EVENTS

- What professional conferences do you regularly attend? In what type of sessions, programs, parties and events do you frequently participate?
- What self development or professional seminars do you attend?
- What type of social, not for profit, or community events do you regularly attend? (Wine and beer festivals, home shows, sporting events) (optional)
- Do you ever attend career building events or job fairs? If so, which ones? (optional)

ORGANIZATIONS

- Of what professional organizations are you a member?
- What social or community organizations do you join? (optional)
- To which university or alumni associations do you belong?

MISCELLANEOUS

- Are there places where you would regularly see outdoor advertising?
- Are there shopping areas where you would see a job opportunity ad?
- Are there places where you eat, go for recreation or entertainment where a recruitment ad might catch your eye?

- What recruitment source caused you to apply for a job at our firm? Your previous job? What element of the ad got your attention (or turned you off)?

- You might consider doing a separate survey of recent college hires to help improve your college recruiting. Try the same for diversity hires.

The "Give Me Five" Referral Program

Who are the five best people you know?
The "Give Me Five" (GM5) program is based on the fact that all of us come across some extremely talented people in our lives, but we never take the time to list them for our recruiters. Employees know who these stars are, but we often need a trigger to stimulate an employee into actually giving us names for our recruiting. In a GM5 program, top performers are asked to think back and remember the names of the 5 very best co-workers, thought leaders, and managers they have ever worked with. Most traditional referral programs require the employee to take the initiative. However, this proactive program sends recruiters periodically to management meetings to ask top performers for names. New hires and even interviewees can be asked the same questions.

Program Goals
1. Develop some immediate leads (that are high quality and pre-assessed).
2. Make every employee a continuous talent scout. Make them "own" recruiting.
3. Develop a "who's who" database of the top talent in your industry/field
4. Utilize it as a prospect database.

Categories of people to bring up (Name stimulators)
Think back and remember the names of the very best *(choose from list below)* you worked with, learned from, admired …
1. Manager
2. Team leader
3. Idea person or innovator
4. Out-of-the-box thinker
5. Problem solver

6. Sales person that beat you time after time in head-to-head competition

7. Student in college who was exceptionally smart and effective

8. Mentor

9. Person under pressure

10. Team player/Co-worker

11. Executive

12. Forecaster (predictor)

13. Technical skilled person

14. International talent

15. People with diverse backgrounds

16. Professor/teacher

17. Customer service person

Put these name "stimulators" on a GM5 form to help stimulate an employee's memory about the best people they ever worked for/with. For each name, also ask about their specific talent and how to contact them.

How to Tell an "A" Player from All the Rest

One of the most difficult tasks facing managers is how to rapidly identify the top candidates from among the average. Although there are few "secret" "A" players, you can speed up the sorting process by compiling a list of key identifiers or commonalities that "A" players consistently have (and that "C" players don't have).

A) Identifying them through their resumes—Elements of a resume that may identify an "A" player include:

- They quantify their accomplishments and job outputs using dollars and numbers.
- They state that they have developed new or innovative processes, systems and approaches.
- They directly compare themselves to their competitors in the industry.
- They cite the tools and skills they used to accomplish their major tasks.
- They mention that projects and task were completed "on-time" and/or "under budget."
- They quantify the success of products (services) they helped to develop in terms of market share, first entry or profitability.
- They use advanced terminology and key buzz words when describing the tools they used to accomplish their job.
- They list examples of promotions, awards or internal or external recognition.
- They cite major firms by name or industry leading statistics as benchmarks.
- They mention a teamwork approach as frequently as individual accomplishments.
- They mention that they took a leadership role in major projects.

B) Assessing/sorting them prior to the interview

Because "A" players do not always possess "A" quality resumes it is often beneficial to do some additional assessment of potential "A" players prior to a formal interview. Some possible tools and strategies for pre-assessment include:

- Ask your current "A" players if they know them and would recommend them.

- Ask your current "A" players to call them, have lunch with them or seek them out at industry events in order to assess them further.

- Ask your recent hires (from their current firm) to give their opinions on their skill level.

- Search the Web, chat rooms/listservers and Usenet for their comments, articles and opinions.

- Search their personal website for examples of their work and indications that they are "A" players.

- Send them a pre-interview questionnaire asking them to develop a list of the characteristics of a top performer in their field. Ask them to identify the top three problems and opportunities facing your industry. This can also be accomplished with an informal telephone interview.

- Call them and ask their advice on steps you should take to solve a critical problem you are facing.

- Send them an e-mail and tell them that you have noted their ideas in an Internet chat room/listserver or an article. Then pose a problem you are facing and ask their opinion on the steps you should take to resolve it.

C) Assessing them during the interview

Consider the following tools in lieu of (or in addition to) traditional interviews:

- Tell them you are looking for problem solvers and ask them to walk you through the steps they would use to solve your toughest problem. Probe why they took that approach. The manager might also ask the candidate for their ideas on a key problem(s) that the candidate will face during their first month on the job.

- Ask them to walk you through the steps they used in solving a difficult problem in their current job.
- Ask them to forecast the major issues and opportunities firms in your industry will face in the next two years.
- In lieu of the traditional interview, ask a senior manager to have a "professional conversation" with them at lunch or during an industry event. Ask the manager to informally assess their skills and abilities.
- Ask the candidate to quantify their outputs and accomplishments.
- Ask candidates if/how they included continuous improvement elements in their major projects.
- Ask candidates to walk you through the steps they take in learning about new issues and solutions.
- Ask candidates to list other top performers and "A" players they know in the industry. See if their list compares favorably with your list. Also use the list given by this and other candidates as a target list for potential recruits.
- Ask candidates to compile their own list of key identifiers they would use to differentiate between "A" and "C" players to see if they know what an "A" player is.
- Remember that pre-assessed employee referrals from your "A" players turn out to be top performers in over 75 percent of cases. So, treat these referrals with less skepticism than your standard candidates.

How to Make Your CEO Your Chief Recruiter

Action Steps for Your CEO

Nothing is more powerful or sends a clearer message to employees than having the CEO announce that he or she is the chief recruiter for the organization. Give the CEO an agenda that lists the things you need him or her to do. Some of the things we recommend include:

1. Have them highlight the importance of employee referrals during their internal talks. Make sure he/she reinforces the need for "every employee to be a recruiter."

2. Have them set aside time for interviews with business and industry journals.

3. Get them to write articles that highlight your great "people programs" and practices.

4. Have them talk at industry and functional trade shows and include parts about your people programs.

5. Have them talk about what a great place your company is to work during their routine PR appearances, as well as at product and customer talks.

6. Have them set aside a certain number of hours per month to call candidates directly or invite them in for visits to encourage them to accept your offers.

7. Involve the CEO directly in orientation, since new hires will generally pass along the excitement this creates to their friends and former colleagues.

8. Ask them directly to ensure that managers are measured and rewarded for great recruiting and retention.

9. Encourage them to write a book about the company and why it is a great place to work.

Making CEO contacts more impactful

CEO calls and visits are powerful but they can be made more powerful if you follow these guidelines. The most effective CEO contacts include these elements:

- The CEO pays a face-to-face visit. (Phone calls are okay but they are a weak second to a visit)
- The CEO thoroughly knows the background and interests of the candidate.
- The CEO makes a pitch that outlines how important the new hire is to the firm's future success as well as an inference that the CEO will be working closely with the candidate.
- The CEO asks the candidate to say yes immediately.
- The CEO shows excitement and enthusiasm and is able to anticipate and answer each question on the spot (without having to "get back to you").
- When appropriate, the CEO calls the spouse and welcomes them to the team
- The CEO asks the new hire to come directly to his office on the first day.

Relationship Recruiting and "Personal Courting"

Relationship Recruiting (also known as Continuous Recruiting) is a strategy that targets the very best currently employed people in high-demand fields. It is a *continuous* process whose goal is to set up a *continuous* pipeline of candidates. It stretches the recruiting process over a period of months (or even years) until the targeted candidate finally decides he is ready to move into the job market (and to your firm).

Steps in the relationship recruiting of Michael Jordan:
Let's look at an example: the goal of hiring a great "player" (like a Michael Jordan). As a top performer, he would most likely not be actively looking for a job during the several week period in which a talent scout (or headhunter) has an open requirement.

1. We start with a continuous process of finding his name as a top performer.

2. We would initially approach him in a professional (non-recruiting) context.

3. We would begin to build a professional (non-recruiting) relationship through phone calls, e-mail exchanges and casual meetings.

4. As this "personal courting" period continues, we would rendezvous at professional meetings, and perhaps invite him to work on joint projects in order to get to know him. We might also comment on his work and introduce him to our team in order to make him familiar with who we are and what opportunities we offer. Because the relationship is based on the trading and exchanging of ideas it would most often be "managed" by a line manager (in their technical area) rather than by an HR recruiter.

5. As opportunities arise at our firm we would make our relationship "targets" aware of them. However, if he was not ready to leave his present firm, we would maintain the relationship until he was ready.

6. Since the goal of relationship recruiting is to build mutual respect to the point where the candidate is convinced that he will "someday work for our firm," the only remaining issue is when that will happen. When the candidate is ready to move, we would negotiate a time that is best for them (and us). An additional goal is getting them to call us exclusively before or when they consider entering the job market.

7. On occasion, if a superstar candidate suddenly decides to change jobs we would literally hire them on the spot (as a "corporate resource"), even though there was no job opening at that time. They would be given a temporary project until there was an opening or a position would be created specifically for them.

Toolkit to help build the relationship:

Here are some of things you can do to build a relationship with a future hire:

✓   Send them an e-mail newsletter/product updates/annual reports.

✓   Offer public technical seminars and invite them to attend.

✓   Get a senior person to mentor them.

✓   Let them sit in on internal company training.

✓   Invite them to open houses and social events.

✓   Periodically comment on their publications, web page, public accolades.

✓   Attend their presentations and comment on their articles.

✓   Call and e-mail them periodically.

✓   Court/hire their mentors and professional friends and team members.

✓   Offer them product discounts, free samples.

✓   Give them an "instant hire" coupon which allows them to skip any final screening interview and start "anytime."

- ✓ Have your CEO call them to say that he/she is interested in working with them.
- ✓ Add them to your personal electronic "Learning Net" in order to exchange ideas.
- ✓ Hire them for a mini project, a weekend, or during their vacation time.
- ✓ Look them up at professional seminars and buy them lunch.
- ✓ "Lend" them some of your products as a beta tester.
- ✓ Put them on your advisory board or involve them in your hiring process as an advisor.
- ✓ Do a behavioral profile to identify when the person is likely to change jobs and what the triggers to movement might be for this individual. Also try to identify their offer "acceptance criteria."
- ✓ If the person is a creative, out-of-the-box thinker (i.e. GenXer) do out-of-the-box things with them (send them concert tickets, a case of a micro-brew, etc.).
- ✓ Use them as a benchmarking source and show them how their ideas contributed to your solution.

How to Identify "Job-Switching Criteria"

Most managers (and recruiters) generally believe that the most important element of recruiting is identifying or finding the *names* of great candidates. In reality, top performers are generally easy to identify and are extremely hard to keep "secret." The real problem occurs once you identify them. That is when you generally find out that they are already happily employed, and they are not readily interested in a new job. They differ from unemployed people in that it takes a lot to get them to even consider a job offer. They can be talked into it, but only if the conditions are perfect.

The criteria that employed people use to assess a new job outside their firm are called "job switching criteria." If you can identify the job switching criteria of currently employed top performers you have added real value to the recruiting equation! Unfortunately because most managers and recruiters focus on resumes in order to recruit candidates, they don't know the job switching criteria because resumes and cover letters do not include the most valuable recruiting information: What are the candidate's "job *switching*" and "job *acceptance*" criteria?

Identifying candidate job switching criteria

Just like in marketing, it is essential that you know your customers "buying criteria" before you attempt to make the sale. Every individual is unique, but you can use standard market research tools to identify the common decision criteria that most individuals in a particular job category use. Some ways of identifying their decision criteria and their relative importance include:

- Focus groups or surveys with your own employees
- Focus groups with employees from many firms (usually done at a trade fair or job fair)
- Directly asking applicants either on your website or during their interviews
- Asking both internal and external recruiters
- Asking new hires on their first day why they said yes

- Asking candidates who rejected your offers, "Why?"

It's important to weight the factors because each does not play an equal role. It is also important to remember that these factors change over time as the economy and the competitive job market change. Incidentally, once you know their decision criteria, it is relatively easy to sell them (just like a salesperson asks, *"What's it going to take to get you to buy _____?"* or, in recruiting terms, *"Under what circumstances would you move forward with this opportunity?"*), providing you have enough flexibility to modify existing jobs to meet the applicant's criteria. Occasionally, HR will take issue with the internal inequity of these offers but if you don't treat people who are in high demand "differently," they won't say yes!

50 Ideas for Recruiting Top Performers Away From Your Competition

"Poaching" is the term recruiters use for directly recruiting (raiding) the employees of another firm. With only 18% of the population actively looking for work, the way to get any volume of talent is to take it directly from other firms.

General "poaching" tools

Identifying who to poach

1. Ask new hires on the first day "Who else is good?" at their previous firm.

2. Ask interviewees who is just as good or better. Offer to hire them as a team.

3. Hire away the competitor's best recruiter (to lessen their competitive impact and to get their "target lists").

4. Use employee referral programs—an effective tool because your employees tend to have extensive networks of friends in similar jobs at other firms.

5. Follow up on your offer "turndowns" from recent years to see if they are still interested.

6. Ask sales people who call on your firm who else is really good at their firm.

7. Identify and track effective service people who fix products used by your firm.

8. Look at rehiring top performers who left your firm (Boomerangs).

9. When benchmarking best practices at other firms, identify top talent.

10. Capture the names of people who buy and comment favorably on your products, services or employees.

11. Capture the names of references provided by applicants.

Which firms to target?

12. Hang out with a banner and recruit in the parking lot/across the street from the company after bad news is announced.

13. Identify firms that have announced recent layoffs, mergers, plant closings and product failures.

14. Target teams that recently completed major projects.

Get friends/mentors to help identify which workers to target

15. Court/hire their mentors, professional friends and team members and woo them to follow.

16. Reward managers who successfully poach workers.

17. Ask internal managers who they informally mentor outside the firm and target the best.

18. Develop a mentor program for top performers outside the firm and use it to woo them.

19. Get ex-employees to act as a key referral source (friends of XYZ company).

20. Offer referral bonuses to non-employees.

21. Offer prizes and rewards to people who are willing to submit an application or come by and participate in an informal interview.

Event/place related tools for poaching

22. Target "user" groups of your products (IT associations).

23. Offer public technical seminars and invite key talent to attend or speak.

24. Use trade shows to learn who the best in the industry are and to find out about your competitors.

25. Buy mailing lists of conference attendees and contact them by phone, mail or e-mail.

26. Speak at events and identify those with great questions.

27. Give your employees who attend conferences "Take a new friend to lunch" coupons for use at conferences.

28. Encourage employees to gather names at airport lounges, rental car buses, shared transportation and on airplanes.

29. Go to the hangout pub or restaurant across the street from your targeted firm and offer the manager an incentive for a "put your business card in the bowl" prize draw if he/she will let you have the business cards from the target firm after it's over.

30. Hold a on-site professional seminar at your firm and assess the attendees.

31. Visit their cafeteria and neighborhood lunch places to get known and to identify the company employees who eat there.

32. Reward employees for attending conferences and capturing the names of impressive people they meet.

Media related tools

33. Scan company press releases and newspaper articles for names of key contributors including those recently promoted.

34. Purchase "who's who" in the industry books to help identify "suspects."

35. Scan the best journals for authors and periodically comment on what they write. Track the names of prominent people mentioned in professional articles.

36. Place billboards on the commute route by your site that demonstrate what a great place it is to work and how "you would be at work now if you worked here."

37. Purchase mailing lists that fit your jobs-demographics and send non-job information to build your image.

38. Target the spouse with at-home direct mail to get them to encourage their spouses to look at your firm.

Web tools for poaching

39. Post a question on listserver and in chat rooms and target those who have great answers.

40. Take advantage of Internet directories and search engines that help identify "white page web sites" to find addressees of the names you have identified.

41. Use portal banner ads for your firm's product and learning sites.

42. Use web cookies to identify visitors from targeted firms to your web site (general and jobs site).

43. Use resume robots/spiders to look for names and personal web sites. Assess and comment on their personal web page.

44. Search company web pages for officer names, contact names or organizational charts.

45. Develop or sponsor web sites that get passive candidates to answer the "I've always wanted to" question in order to capture names and aspirations.

46. Identify and target people that use Usenet groups.

47. Post technical articles and accomplishments on your web page to show the quality of your talent and capture the names of people who comment on or read them.

48. Utilize name-finder web sites or firms to capture the names of employees who have developed patents and technology advances.

49. Identify "old" (1 yr. old or more) resumes on the net (now-employed people who may be ready to look again).

50. Have employees join social networking sites like MySpace, Facebook, and others so that they can electronically network with the friends and peers of former colleagues, college friends, etc.

Applicant's Bill of Rights

Treating applicants better is becoming a hot issue again, just like it was during the last war for talent. An improving economy means that if you want high application and offer acceptance rates, you need to begin to pay attention to your "candidate experience."

"Applicants are not stupid. If you treat them harshly when they are essentially 'guests' at your company, they will automatically assume that you will treat them even worse if they become employees."

Compiling an Applicant's Bill of Rights

There is no standard format or magic formula for developing an applicant's Bill of Rights. Design your recruiting process so that it reflects the way you would like to be treated if you were applying for a job. Make a list of your goals for applicant treatment and develop an individual promise or "right" to fit each of these customer service goals.

A SAMPLE APPLICANT'S BILL OF RIGHTS

Here is a sample Bill of Rights that might be utilized by a large but conservative Fortune 500 corporation with a high-volume of applicants.

1. To treat applicants like customers and to keep them informed on a periodic basis.

2. To ensure that job descriptions, Want Ads, web site information and brochures contain accurate and current information about the job responsibilities and the required skills, so that applicants get a realistic job preview.

3. To acknowledge the candidate's right to privacy and to ensure that any information provided is not utilized outside the selection process.

4. To immediately remove any "already filled" jobs and never to post "ghost jobs" (where no real job exists) on the web site.

5. To limit the number of interviews to a reasonable number, so that the applicant does not suffer through "death by interview."

6. To respect an applicant's current employer and job-related time constraints by making a good-faith effort to provide interview times and locations that fit the applicant's needs.

7. To make a fair offer within the range of the applicant's expectations the very first time. We promise to play no games by initially making "lowball' offers.

8. To ensure that we meet both the spirit and the letters-of-the-laws on discrimination that protect applicant rights, and to design and maintain a process that provides diverse individuals with equal opportunity.

9. To provide reasonable access whenever possible at all phases of the selection process for people with disabilities and special needs, including readers, Braille materials and signers where appropriate.

10. To solicit feedback from applicants and evaluate how well they are treated according to this Bill of Rights.

Recruiting Effectiveness Questionnaire

A new-hire questionnaire for improving recruiting processes

Now that you have joined our firm you are in a unique position to further help us build a winning team. Please be frank and help us improve our recruiting processes and bring in more top talent.

A) Improving the process
What **convinced you to apply** to XYZ Company? (Check all that fit)

I heard good things about the management practices at XYZ through:
- ☐ 1) Articles in industry publications
- ☐ 2) Articles in functional publications
- ☐ 3) Articles in newspapers
- ☐ 4) TV or radio show
- ☐ 5) Talks at conferences and seminars
- ☐ 6) Benchmarking studies citing best practices and firms
- ☐ 7) A current employee referred me
- ☐ 8) The web site content convinced me
- ☐ 9) A newspaper ad/job posting convinced me
- ☐ 10) A "job board" web site job posting convinced me
- ☐ 11) Other reason

_____

What were the key factors that finally convinced you to **accept** our offer?
- ☐ 1) Reputation of XYZ as a good place to work
- ☐ 2) A friend convinced me to
- ☐ 3) Pay
- ☐ 4) Benefits
- ☐ 5) The team
- ☐ 6) Flexibility
- ☐ 7) My managers and their style
- ☐ 8) Other _____

What part of the recruiting and screening process worked best (impressed you)? Explain why for each item:

1.
2.
3.

What part of the recruiting, screening, and interview process could use some improvement (or even made you uncomfortable)? Explain why for each:

1.
2.
3.

B) Other firms you seriously considered

What other firms did you seriously consider? (Please list in descending order of your interest)

	Firm	Superior element of their firm?
1.		
2.		
3.		
4.		

C) Will you help us identify other top performers like you?

Who else should we recruit from your former firm? State their job and strengths (please list in descending order of their value as recruits). A referral bonus may be paid to you if one of your referrals is hired within 6 months.

1.
2.
3.
4.
5.

Will you help us recruit them? (Put a Yes/or No by each name)

"Understanding You Better" Questionnaire

Help us understand you and how you prefer to be managed
Employees at our company have a shared responsibility (along with their managers) to help ensure that you are as content, motivated, and productive as possible. Because you are new to this position and/or the organization, you can help us understand how to manage and motivate you so that you can do "the best work of your life." Although this form is an important first step, it is imperative that you continue to help your manager and your team leader understand what your goals are and how we can best help you reach them.

A) Things that motivate me and that will increase my productivity
Please provide me <u>MORE OF</u> the following:

Recognition and rewards (list examples)
1.
2.
3.

Learning opportunities
1.
2.
3.

Exposure and contacts
1.
2.
3.

Work experiences and projects (time allocation)
1.
2.
3.

Tools and resources
1.
2.
3.

Things I'd like to try
1.
2.
3.

Other
1.
2.
3.
4.
5.

B) Things that frustrate me and decrease my productivity
Please when possible provide me <u>LESS OF</u> the following (For example—approvals, reports, meetings, work assignments, co-workers, scheduling, equipment, etc.)
1.
2.
3.
4.
5.
6.
7.
8.
9.
10.

Even though you accepted our offer, we would still like to know what are your initial concerns about this new job? (Please list in descending order of importance)

1.
2.
3.

Why did you quit your last job? (So we can try to avoid similar issues)

1.
2.
3.

Expectations

Where would you like to be in your career in three years? The list could include job titles, who you report to, responsibilities, or experiences (Please list in descending order of importance).

1.
2.
3.

Easy-to-Use Retention Tools for Managers

Top 10 things an individual manager can do *now* to impact retention:

1. Identify and make a list of the top performers and key people you want to retain.

2. Ask key people why they stay and what frustrates them. Do a more-of/less-of list with each.

3. Ask key people to stay and ask them to warn you before they considering leaving.

4. Develop an individual challenge plan for every employee. Realize that employees rank it #1.

5. Educate each employee so they understand they have a shared responsibility to help their manager understand what motivates and frustrates them as well as what their aspirations and the key aspects of their "dream" job are. Two-way communication needs to be established.

6. Tell each employee that they have the right to demand the "big 6" from their manager ...

   • Communication

   • Recognition and reward

   • Challenge

   • Growth and learning

   • Knowing their job makes a difference

   • Some control over their job

7. Ask other employees and managers "Who is at risk of leaving?"

8. Institute "part-time" job rotations for full time employees and short term assignment programs.

9. Make a list for every key employee of "What motivates you to do your best work?"

10. Create a list of key employees who are "overdue" for recognition, promotion, training, etc.

REFERENCES

Adams, Michael. *Better Happy Than Rich?* Penguin Books, Toronto. 2000

Adler, Lou. *Thinking Outside the Box First Requires Getting Out of It.* Electronic Recruiting Exchange. Sept 10, 2004

Adler, Lou. *Hire With Your Head.* John Wiley & Sons, Hoboken, NJ. 2002.

Buckingham, Marcus, & Coffman, Curt. *First, Break All the Rules.* Simon & Schuster, New York. 1999.

CBC Newsworld, "The Way We Work." www.cbc.ca/news/work

Collins, Jim. *Good to Great.* HarperCollins, New York, 2001

Cork, David. *The Pig and the Python.* Stoddart Publishing, Toronto. 1996

Covey, Stephen. *The 7 Habits of Highly Effective People.* Simon & Schuster, New York. 1990

Creeley, David. *Return on Investment in Talent Management, a Human Capital Institute position paper.* Sept 2004

Dearlove, Des. *Business the Bill Gates Way.* Capstone Publishing. 1999

Foot, David. *Boom, Bust & Echo 2000: Profiting from the Demographic Shift in the New Millennium.* Stoddart Publishing, Toronto. 1999

Hammer, Michael & Champy, James. *Re-engineering the Corporation. A Manifesto for Business Revolution*. HarperCollins Publishers, New York. 2001

Johnson, Spencer. *Who Moved My Cheese?* G.P. Putnam's Sons, New York. 2000

McKinsey & Company Inc, Michaels et al., *The War For Talent*, Harvard Bus School Press, Boston. 2001

Peters, Tom. *Re-imagine! Business Excellence in a Disruptive Age*. Dorling Kindersley (Penguin), London. 2003

Pink, Dan. *Free Agent Nation*. Warner Books, New York. 2002

Sharma, Robin. *The Greatness Guide*. HarperCollins, Toronto. 2006

Sullivan, John. *Rethinking Strategic HR*. CCH Incorporated. 2003.

Sullivan, John. *HR Metrics the World Class Way*. Kennedy Information. 2003

Welch, Jack and Byrne, John. *Straight From the Gut*. Warner Books, New York. 2001

Wheeler, Kevin. *Defining Talent in 5 Steps*. Electronic Recruiting Exchange. December 8, 2004

Worzel, Richard. *Who Owns Tomorrow? 7 Secrets for the Future of Business*. Viking Canada, Toronto. 2003

ABOUT THE AUTHORS

DR. JOHN SULLIVAN:
Dr. Sullivan currently serves as a Professor of Management Program at San Francisco State University. Formerly he was the chief talent officer for Agilent Technologies (the 43,000-employee Hewlett Packard spin-off). Sullivan has been described as one of the leading strategists in the field of human resources around the globe. He has advised more than 300 corporations worldwide, helping leading firms identify, test, and perfect the best hiring practices of tomorrow. Firms he has advised include: Microsoft, Starbucks, Nike, Intel, GE, HP, Charles Schwab, BMW, Pepsi, Google, Nestle Foods, AOL/Netscape and Oracle. His work has been translated into more than 26 languages. Over the last five years Dr. Sullivan has penned more than 700 articles and five books on subjects ranging from metrics to strategic planning for the human resource function. His work on e-hr was dubbed "brilliant" by management guru Tom Peters and *Fast Company* magazine coined him the "Michael Jordan of Hiring." Sullivan lives with his wife near San Francisco. He can be reached through his website at: www.drjohnsullivan.com

GREG FORD
Greg Ford is a vice-president at one of Canada's largest employment search firms, David Aplin Recruiting, selected as one of Canada's 50 Best Managed Companies in 2008. Clients include dozens of Fortune 500 companies such as Microsoft, IBM, GE, American Express, Coca Cola, Bell, Deloitte and more. As well, Ford was an instructor of business writing and communications at one of the largest colleges in Western Canada. His articles have been published in national magazines, and he has spoken at conferences and training seminars. Along with twenty years of business experience in recruiting, training, marketing and communications, Ford holds two undergraduate degrees and is currently completing a Masters degree in Adult Education and Workplace Learning. He lives with his wife and three children in Vancouver, Canada and can be reached at: gford@aplin.com

978-0-595-48401-0
0-595-48401-8

Printed in the United States
105826LV00002B/1-102/P